THE VALIANT FEW

THE MACMILLAN BATTLE BOOKS are prepared
under the general editorship of Edward R. Sammis

THE VALIANT FEW

Crisis at the Alamo

By LON TINKLE

THE MACMILLAN COMPANY, NEW YORK
COLLIER–MACMILLAN LIMITED, LONDON

General Sam Houston, Governor of Texas, as he looked in 1861

1

The Prologue

GENERAL Sam Houston, lying stretched out on a Mexican blanket under a great live oak, forgot for a moment the pain in his bullet-torn right leg. While Texas Army Surgeon Alexander Ewing tested the ankle and calf for bone splinters, Sam composed a letter to his good friend, Andrew Jackson, then the President of the United States.

Houston dated his letter April 22, 1836, and under it added "San Jacinto." But he doubted whether the President would find the name on any map then available in the White House.

At noon on the 21st, Texas had belonged to Mexico—as it had ever since the Spanish explorer Pineda first discovered it in 1519, just twenty-seven years after Columbus' first voyage. By nightfall of that day, the territory could claim to be the Republic of Texas. A decisive battle had been fought, and victory had been achieved.

Houston himself had almost been a casualty. Early in the fighting, his white horse, Saracen, had been shot from under him; he called for a new mount, but that, too, was downed. Finally, on the third try, the Mexicans got Sam himself. But he charged ahead. When the moment of victory was in hand, he fainted into the arms of his aide, Major George Hockley.

And now, twenty-four hours later, Surgeon Ewing was dressing the wound again. He was worried. It looked as though lockjaw might set in. Ewing ordered Houston to leave at once for New Orleans, where he could have his foot properly treated. Sam shook his head stubbornly; he had unfinished business at San Jacinto.

The Texans had killed, wounded or captured nearly every soldier on the Mexican side. But one man who got away, riding off on a black horse, was President-General Antonio López de Santa Anna. He happened to be the man most wanted by the Texans. If Santa Anna were to rejoin the other two wings of his army, then the Texans' triumph would be an empty one.

At that very moment, five Texas scouts rode in with a new prisoner. He was dressed like a peon, except for the fact that he was wearing red carpet slippers. He was tall for a Mexican, five feet ten, and straight as a pine tree.

A huddle of Mexican soldiers watched the captive get off his horse. After a moment of startled surprise, they yelled out in their excitement, "*El presidente! Viva el presidente!*"

A cursory glance told Sam Houston that General Santa Anna, his most sought-after prize, was in his hands.

Santa Anna made no further attempt to conceal his identity from his captors.

"I place myself," he said in Spanish, standing at attention, "at the disposal of the brave General Houston." Then he added, "That man may consider himself born to no common destiny who has conquered the Napoleon of the West. And now it remains for him to be generous to the vanquished."

Leaning on the shoulder of an aide to favor his wounded leg, Houston fixed on Santa Anna a look of the utmost contempt, and said, "You should have remembered that at the Alamo!"

The capture of General Santa Anna

The Texas Territory

The capture of Santa Anna marked the end of the Texas War of Independence. On the plain of San Jacinto, the Mexican General had been brought face to face with the truth that awaits all dictators, namely that, soon or late, somewhere, sometime, men will decide that liberty is worth dying for. Six weeks earlier, at the Alamo, 187 men stood by this decision and so altered the course of history. What drove them to resist with their lives had its origins, as we shall see, a long way back in the past.

For centuries, Texas had been a thorny problem. First of all, to whom did it belong? Although Spanish explorers had discovered it, the French claimed the land on the grounds that La Salle had colonized it, beginning in 1685. Neither nation much cared; it scarcely mattered who owned Texas, for nobody wanted to live in it. Except for a few padres, the territory was populated only by Indians and herds of buffalo. The Catholic friars had made many heroic attempts to Christianize these Indians and to that end had founded many missions. But the results, though paid for in saintly devotion, were discouragingly slight.

The first real crisis over Texas developed in 1803 with the Louisiana Purchase. Agents for France, thinking their claim was valid, led Thomas Jefferson to believe that the land that he had bought included Texas, all the way down to the Rio Grande.

In 1819, under the treaty with Spain, the United States formally gave up all claim to Texas in exchange for Spain's surrender of its claim to Florida.

To Spanish Mexico, the sole value of this empty land was to serve as a buffer between that country and the rapidly expanding United States.

Then, in 1821, a brilliant young lawyer, Stephen F. Austin, who had moved to Texas from Missouri, persuaded the Mexican Government to invite Americans to come there to help develop the land.

This seemed a sensible arrangement for all concerned. The Americanos, experienced farmers, could not only make Texas safe, but prosperous. The cost to Spanish Mexico would be nothing, the only price being some land that nobody wanted anyway.

As for the Americans, they had an incentive to go. Many of them were suffering from the financial panic of 1819, which had ruined about half the population of the United States, wiping out farms, closing banks, bankrupting businesses. Austin and his father had been among the victims of this panic.

In the year that Austin appeared, Mexico won its independence from Spain. The new government was glad to get these volunteer citizens to redeem the Texas wilderness. As

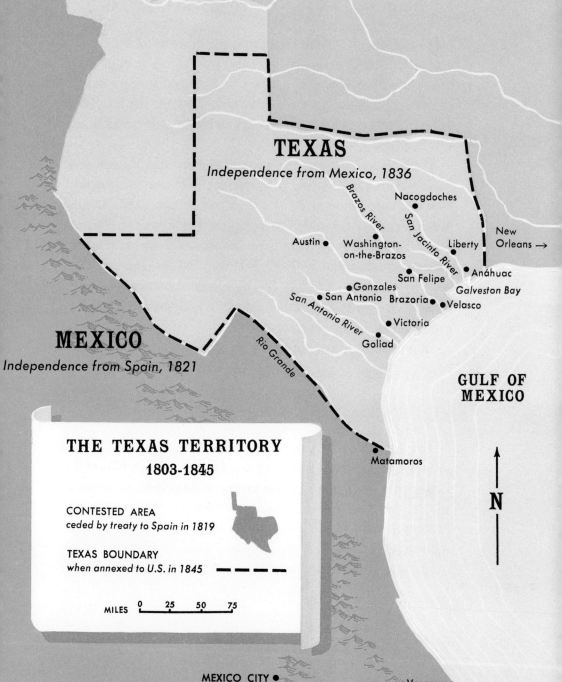

LOUISIANA PURCHASE

Purchase from France, 1803

TEXAS

Independence from Mexico, 1836

Nacogdoches

Brazos River

San Jacinto River

New Orleans →

Austin ●

Washington-on-the-Brazos

Liberty ●

San Felipe ●

Anáhuac ●

Gonzales ●

San Antonio ●

Brazoria ●

Galveston Bay

San Antonio River

● Velasco

● Victoria

Goliad ●

Rio Grande

MEXICO

Independence from Spain, 1821

GULF OF
MEXICO

Matamoros ●

THE TEXAS TERRITORY
1803-1845

CONTESTED AREA
ceded by treaty to Spain in 1819

TEXAS BOUNDARY
when annexed to U.S. in 1845 — — —

MILES 0 25 50 75

N

MEXICO CITY ●

Veracruz ●

a reward, each settler was given title to about four thousand acres of free land. Thirty thousand newcomers arrived in the next ten years.

Stephen F. Austin

Austin, slight of build, patient and diplomatic by nature, was well educated for his day. His father, Connecticut-born, had spent a lifetime on the move, making and losing fortunes in mining; but he sent his son back East for his boyhood schooling, then to a new university in Kentucky, called Transylvania.

Texas at once began to attract Americans. Austin sent back reports representing the province as the new Garden of Eden, almost untouched, its soil as rich as any in the United States. Austin dreamed of developing Texas into an agricultural paradise. But the next three leaders to come, men whose names were to shine in Texas history, had no interest whatever in farming. They were men already known on the frontier as public figures, as wanderers, fighters and adventurers.

Their names were Sam Houston, James Bowie and William Barret Travis.

Three Adventurers

The first to arrive was Jim Bowie. He had, in fact, been in and out of Texas since 1819. Already rich while still a young man, Bowie had an incurable wanderlust. At an early age he had become nationally famous for his prowess in hand-to-hand encounters with the desperadoes who infested the southern trails.

He was also known as the inventor of the Bowie knife,

Jim Bowie   *Stephen F. Austin*

which was soon to become a standard item in every frontiersman's equipment. The knife had a blade almost two feet long
with the cutting edge on both sides of the tip and a wide
handle guard, which made it effective not only as a tool but
as a fighting weapon. (Jim never made the knife himself, but
he did make the wooden model for it, which he then gave to
James Black, a master metal smith in Arkansas Territory,
who made its replica in steel.)

Bowie was a contradictory character, the six-foot, red-
haired embodiment of personal courage, but also soft-spoken,
gentle and chivalrous. During his youth he was reputed to
have ridden alligators and lassoed wild mustangs, but he was
also at home in New Orleans society.

Bowie had come to Texas seeking gold and silver, but he
found instead a beautiful girl named Ursula Veramendi. In
1831 he married her and settled down.

Jim shortly went into business as a partner with his father-in-law, Juan Veramendi. Between them they concocted grandiose plans for building cotton gins and textile mills, and, at the same time, selling millions of acres of Texas land to new settlers. The more settlers, they reasoned, the more customers.

The second of the trio to arrive was William Barret Travis, another fiery redhead, who came to Texas in 1831 at the age of twenty-two. Born in South Carolina of a prominent family, Travis grew up in Alabama, where he studied law and also taught school. He later married one of his prettiest pupils. The marriage, however, was not a happy one. In time Travis, saddened by his domestic misfortune, moved west to make a new start in life. In New Orleans he met Sam Houston, and they became fast friends.

Houston, an impressive giant of a man who stood six feet two in his stocking feet, was the last of the three to come.

When Sam was twenty-one an incident occurred which was to shape his life. While fighting against the Creek Indians in Alabama in the campaign of 1814, Sam was wounded in the leg by an arrow. General Andrew Jackson, under whose command he was serving, dressed his wound and sternly forbade him to rejoin the fighting. In consequence, a friendship began which lasted throughout their lives.

When Jackson became President, he sponsored Sam Houston's political career in Tennessee, where Sam was first elected to the Congress, then to the governorship of the state. But

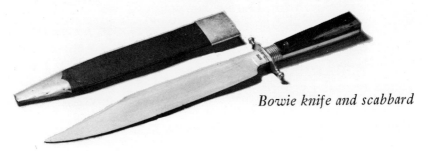

Bowie knife and scabbard

William Barret Travis
(*Daughters of the*
Republic of Texas
at the Alamo,
San Antonio, Texas)

domestic difficulties intervened. After a few weeks of marriage, his young bride deserted him. In chagrin, he resigned his governorship and went to live in Arkansas Territory with the Cherokee Indians, his old friends and comrades, whose cause he had defended in Washington.

A man who loved nature as well as soldiering and politics, Houston came to the more open wilderness of Texas in 1832. Perhaps he came to act as a secret agent for Jackson, perhaps to start his political career all over again. His ambitions may have been dormant, but they certainly were not dead. When he crossed the Red River into Texas, a friend who had accompanied him to this point gave him a razor as a parting gift. Houston is reported to have said: "Mark my words. Some day this razor will shave the chin of the president of a great republic."

Sam Houston, on his first visit, liked everything he saw in Texas—with the exception of Stephen F. Austin. Houston, dramatic and physically overpowering, often referred with heavy sarcasm to the number one Texas leader as "the little gentleman."

The dislike was mutual. The presence in Texas of Houston, Bowie and Travis gave Austin some concern. He suspected, not without reason, that they cherished dreams of empire. He was aware that they had been sending back to the United States glowing accounts calculated to attract more settlers into the territory, further stimulating the "Texas fever" which was sweeping the States.

Mexico was already suspicious of the intentions of its powerful neighbor to the north. And when Jackson unsuccessfully tried to buy Texas from Mexico, offering on his last bid as much as $5 million, the mistrust became acute.

Andrew Jackson leads the 1814 fight against the Creek Indians.

Why was the United States so eager to buy Texas? Did the country, embarked on a westward march, see this vast territory as a steppingstone by means of which it could one day extend its boundaries all the way to the west coast? Was the fevered push for colonization all part of a deep-laid plot? Mexico was beginning to regret having opened Texas to settlement by Americans. But it was already too late.

Two Prisoners

In 1831, the year that Travis arrived in Texas, the first real crisis occurred between the "Anglo" colonists and the Mexican Government. This was the tenth year after a settlement had first been established in the territory. By means of new laws passed in April, 1830, Mexico had forbidden further emigration from the United States.

To enforce these new laws, which also called for the levying of duties and the collection of taxes, Mexico sent a garrison of 300 men to Anáhuac, the chief Texan port at the time, on Galveston Bay. In command was one Captain John Davis Bradburn, a Kentuckian who had volunteered his services to Mexico in its war of liberation from Spain, and then had stayed on to serve in the Mexican Army.

Because of this continued allegiance, Bradburn now found himself in the ironic position of collecting taxes from his fellow Americans. A bully by nature, Bradburn aroused the ire of the Texans with his arrogance.

Travis and others retaliated by tormenting him with pranks that made him look ridiculous. Brandburn decided to put an end to this. He clapped Travis and another young lawyer, Patrick Jack, into prison.

Friends of the two quickly rallied a relief force at Anáhuac. Their first act was to capture a few Mexican guards in order to force Bradburn to exchange them for Travis and Jack. Bradburn agreed; but he demanded delivery of his own men first. Once they were handed over, he refused to keep his part of the bargain, ordering instead that Travis and Jack be tied down and horsewhipped. The Texans were outraged.

For the first time events were taking a serious turn. Then Bradburn announced that he was sending his prisoners to Veracruz for military trial. Travis and Jack wouldn't stand a chance. The Texans knew that if they did not stop Bradburn now, they would henceforth be helpless victims of Mexican tyranny. There was no time to lose.

The Brazoria Cannon

At Anáhuac Bradburn had built himself a new fort. The Texans had no hope of taking it because they didn't have any cannon. But there happened to be one over at the settlement of Brazoria on the Brazos River, a hundred miles to the west. Some of the Texans at Anáhuac decided to go after it. The others withdrew a few miles north and pitched camp at Turtle Bayou, there to await the gun's arrival.

The quickest means of getting the cannon to Anáhuac was by boat. Luckily, a fine large schooner, belonging to Captain John G. Rowland, was then lying at mooring in the Brazos River.

When the Texans commandeered his craft, Captain Rowland was absent. The boat's mate, a Northerner, kindly offered to help the Texans work the vessel, but he said flatly that he wanted no part of any fighting; he was a poor man with a large family to support back home.

The cannon aboard, the volunteer crew set sail down river. Only one hazard presented itself. The ship would have to run the gantlet past the Mexican garrison at Velasco, 25 miles

downstream, where Colonel Francisco Ugartechea commanded 150 men.

The fort at Velasco was circular, built of logs and sand
and surrounded by a stockade. Its most formidable weapon
was a nine-pounder, standing a good bit higher than the
outside wall. A two-foot parapet had been built around the
cannon to protect those who manned it.

The Texans' strategy centered on this detail. If a surprise
force were to gain the cover of the outside walls, the cannon
could not be turned downward to shoot them.

John Austin (no kin to Stephen) led two units to attack
the fort by land from the south and from the north at the
same time. Under cover of darkness the boat would be ready
to streak past when the garrison had been diverted by the
fire of the attacking Texans.

The assault was carefully planned. Austin improvised port-
able defenses by battening together four-foot lengths of
lumber; the attacking force also carried tools for digging
trenches and embankments.

On the night of June 25, 1832, the two hundred or so

An American cannon used during the Texas War of Independence

Texans scrambled ashore. The land units and the boat reached their rendezvous just above the fort without incident. Firing would commence at daybreak.

The Fight at Velasco

Undetected, Austin's detachments set up their breastworks as planned, about thirty yards from the fort. The men had been ordered to work in total silence. They had even taken precautions against recklessness or accident by emptying their guns beforehand.

All, that is, but one man, Edward Robinson, a volunteer from Brazoria. Unable to bear the enforced silence, he let out a war whoop shortly after midnight and took a pot shot at the fort. His shot revealed the Texans' position. It also aroused the startled Mexicans who speedily turned their artillery pieces against the Texan breastworks. These were not strong enough to withstand the crashing balls. Robinson, who gave the alarm, was the first to die.

But the Texans at their posts waited for daylight to reveal the targets for their rifles. Seven of them were killed, a good many wounded. As the dawn brightened, Austin's sharpshooters took aim and nearly halted the Mexican fire. Then, abruptly, the fight was interrupted by a heavy downpour. The Texan land units used this respite to retreat to the boat, where a doctor and medical supplies were waiting.

"Captain" Russell, in charge of the Texans on board, had used up most of his ammunition when Robinson's excitability had let the cat out of the bag. The boat's moorings had been shot away. She had drifted idly onto the bank, where she lay, hard ashore, two hundred yards from the fort.

Then the rain stopped, as suddenly as it had begun. Colonel Ugartechea started blasting away at the ship with his nine-

pounder. But Texas rifle fire cut down every man who appeared to light the cannon. Finally, Ugartechea himself
climbed up to the parapet. He was a brave man, well-known
to the Texans. Recognizing him, they gave the Colonel an
immense cheer; then they started shooting again.

By ten o'clock Ugartechea had had enough. His losses
appalled him. He hoisted a white flag.

With the obstacle eliminated, the Texans could proceed to
Anáhuac. Ugartechea agreed to retreat with his garrison
below the Rio Grande. One ball from his nine-pounder had
pierced the ship's side during the night. Ironically, it had
also hit the Northern mate who, by agreement, had gone
below decks for safety. He had died instantly.

John Austin's casualty list reported one man killed on the
boat, "name unknown." The Texans' first act after victory
was to raise funds for the mate's family.

A Brief Peace

The cannon never had to be used. Before the schooner
reached Anáhuac, Bradburn had been relieved of his command and the quarrel settled by debate rather than by gunfire.

Some of the colonists persuaded Colonel José de las Piedras,
senior officer in charge of the garrison at Nacogdoches, to
investigate Bradburn's injustices. Piedras moved in. He listened to complaints, then he freed Travis and Jack, and
ordered Bradburn to return to Mexico. Bradburn, fearful
that he might be tarred and feathered, stole away secretly.

Thus ended the Battle of Anáhuac, 1832—so called although the fighting had taken place at Fort Velasco.

The Texans referred to this act of rebellion as their Boston
Tea Party.

Mexican President-General Antonio López de Santa Anna

The participants had only luck to thank that they were not punished.

But just then the trouble in Texas seemed like a small matter indeed to the Mexicans. Their government was torn by conspiracy, counterplots and confusion. The strongest man in the nation, able to make and break presidents, was General Santa Anna. Just now, he was plotting to bring to an end the short rule of General Bustamante who had come to power by revolt. Santa Anna was about to take over the government himself.

At the time, Santa Anna seemed to be a man committed to the principles of democracy. He was known as the upholder of Mexico's famed Constitution of 1824, modeled closely on that of its sister republic, the United States.

But at heart he was a dictator; as soon as he got full power he showed his true colors. With characteristic humility he began to refer to himself as the "Napoleon of the West." As matters turned out he meant it. But briefly, in 1832 and 1833, he and the Texans were friends.

Provocation

The battle, again involving Travis, had to be repeated at exactly the same place, at Anáhuac, in 1835, before Santa Anna was goaded to retaliatory action.

By then it was clear that this gifted, vainglorious opportunist was interested only in personal power. In May, 1834, after assuming the presidency, he scrapped the Constitution of 1824, dissolved the state legislatures and destroyed his adversaries wherever he could run them down.

The Constitution had guaranteed the Texans separate statehood once the province had become prosperous and sufficiently developed. In 1833, the settlers had sent Austin to present a petition requesting fulfillment of the guarantee. Santa Anna clapped him into jail and kept him there for almost two years before shipping him back to Texas.

All that this move accomplished was to turn Austin, who had been the most sympathetic to Mexico among all the Texan leaders, against Santa Anna at last.

A great banquet was held to celebrate Austin's return. But Austin was grim. Speaking at that occasion, he announced: "Our only recourse is war."

Early in 1835 Santa Anna had restored the irksome measures which the 1832 rebellion had nullified. Santa Anna dispatched his dandified brother-in-law, General Martín Perfecto de Cós, to make sure that laws were obeyed this time. Cós arrived with 1,000 men to swell the numbers already in position at the nine reinstated garrison forts.

The new captain assigned to Bradburn's former brick fort at Anáhuac was the young Antonio Tenorio, a reasonable and agreeable man. His job was to try to stop the smuggling and to seek to collect duties on the supplies coming in to the colonists from New Orleans, which was their only real source of farm tools, food, clothing and sundries.

One day, two of Travis' closest friends received a big shipment of goods. They failed to make a declaration, claiming that they didn't intend to pay taxes on the necessities of life, and Tenorio ordered their arrest. A fight ensued. Tenorio's agents were knocked down. But Travis' friends were jailed finally, while they awaited trial.

Travis Calls a Meeting

The news of the arrest reached Travis while he was at San Felipe, principal settlement of the Austin colony. He

A view of 19th century New Orleans—the "mother of Texas"

called a town meeting and, over the protests of the cautious, his "war party" voted to drive out Santa Anna's soldiers and the tax collectors, just as they had done in 1832.

This was a much more serious decision than the one that had brought on the first Anáhuac skirmish. Santa Anna himself was now the enemy; he would become an implacable one.

Travis, with twenty-five men, set out overland to the western shore of Galveston Bay. From there he sailed across to Anáhuac at night. The Mexicans were awakened by a fusillade. Supposing from the noise that a whole navy was assembled, Captain Tenorio surrendered without a fight.

Tenorio agreed, as Ugartechea had, to leave Texas. The Texans escorted the departing Mexicans up the bayou. It was all very amiable.

Santa Anna was the only one who refused to forget it. He declared that he would come to Texas in person to punish such insolence.

Preparations for War

About this time, the Texans intercepted a letter from Santa Anna to his Texas command. In it, he called for the military trial of Travis and half-a-dozen other leaders of the revolt. This was a decree of death. The seriousness of Travis' second assault on Anáhuac was now only too clear.

Santa Anna meant war. The Texans felt they had no choice but to resist.

A convention was set for late October. Austin urged that official action be taken to achieve unity, and that a volunteer army be formed at once with the immediate objective of walling off Santa Anna's emissary, General Cós, and his men in San Antonio. This part of the province was known as "Spanish Texas"; the eastern half as "Anglo Texas."

The westernmost settlement of Anglo Texas was Gonzales, sixty-seven miles east of San Antonio. Gonzales became the rallying point. Here the volunteers began streaming in. They promptly elected Stephen F. Austin their commander, by unanimous vote.

Sam Houston was skeptical of all this. One of the few who had been in battle, he had little confidence in the ability of these raw recruits, experienced only in shooting wild turkey and deer, to resist the Mexicans. They would have to be drilled, disciplined and equipped with muskets and cannon, with supplies and ammunition. Especially cannon.

The first encounter between the two sides took place over the possession of one of these fieldpieces.

October 2, 1835

General Cós sent word to Colonel Ugartechea, now in command of the Mexican garrison at San Antonio, to retrieve from the citizens of Gonzales a weapon which the government had given them earlier to protect themselves against Indian attack.

As the token detachment approached Gonzales, the Texans hoisted a white flag on which was lettered, "Come and Take It!" (The flag had been made from the wedding dress of the daughter of Green DeWitt, friend of Austin and founder of the settlement.)

Infuriated, Ugartechea sent back another and larger force of 200 men. The Texans were ready for them. Under cover of darkness, they hauled their ordnance into place on the riverbank opposite the Mexican camp. Next morning, at first light, they fired. The sudden boom sent the Mexicans scrambling all the way back to San Antonio.

This brief struggle on October 2, 1835, over a single six-pounder cannon, is often called "The Lexington of the Texas Revolution." General Cós had been defied; war had begun.

More Volunteers

The news of the Mexican rout at Gonzales ran like wild-fire through the United States. It brought in more volunteers from among the colonists; and later hundreds more from the States. From Pennsylvania to Georgia, from New York and Boston to New Orleans, friends, kinsmen, politicians, newspaper editors and others "back home" organized "Help Texas" meetings; they raised money and bought munitions; volunteers formed companies to set out "to fight for freedom in Texas."

In Mobile, Alabama, on October 20th, such a company was formed by one James Bonham, then twenty-eight years old, a boyhood friend of Travis'. More was to be heard of Bonham later.

A week before, the New Orleans Committee for Texas had enlisted a hundred Americans, lured by posters placed all over town, and had raised $10,000 at one meeting. The first 50 volunteers were given free rifles by Adolphus Sterne, German-born merchant at Nacogdoches. This was the first company of New Orleans Greys, named for the color of the uniforms they found in a warehouse. They left for Gonzales next day, proceeding by boat upriver to Nacogdoches where they were to be furnished with horses. A second company of New Orleans Greys, numbering 100 men, left a little later by ship out of New Orleans headed for a Texas gulf port.

No more than a thousand or so volunteers reached Texas before the battle of San Jacinto in April, 1836. Many came after that; but they arrived too late to help in the fight against Santa Anna.

Fort Goliad

On the very day the first company of Greys left New Orleans, a small Texas unit led by "Old Ben" Milam, a colonizer like Austin, attacked the Mexican garrison at Fort Goliad, a stronghold on the river 100 miles below San Antonio. Milam caught them off guard and put the 50 men to flight. The officer in charge, his soldiers having deserted him, surrendered, yielding the Texans two great prizes: possession of a fort that cut off Cós's supply line from the Gulf; and supplies the Texans needed desperately, including $10,000 in cash and a fine stand of rifles with ammunition. Ben Milam set out for Gonzales at once with the loot. Austin was now able to march on San Antonio with 600 men.

A Gamble

To reconnoiter approaches to San Antonio, Austin dispatched a force under the command of Jim Bowie and Colonel James Fannin. Fannin was an important recent recruit from the States. Georgia-born, he had spent two years at West Point, where he left under a cloud for getting into fights. Fannin, who had come to Texas as a planter, was a colorful man with a great gift for disciplining others but none for disciplining himself. Houston admired him; Austin remained doubtful.

Bowie and Fannin made camp on October 26th at the old abandoned Mission Concepción, just a few miles below San Antonio. Next morning a heavy fog veiled the sun. Bowie and others, watching the fog float, wondered how long it would be before the sun steamed it away. Suddenly, out of the mists emerged about two hundred of Cós's crack troops, lancers accompanied by a cannon.

Ben Milam

This time it was the Mexicans who had sprung the surprise. Jim Bowie took command. A sudden rift in the fog revealed the cannon trained on them only eighty yards away. But the clearing weather also rendered the cannon useless; for it stood in the open, and everyone attempting to fire it was picked off by the Texas rifles. Then Bowie, a gambling man, decided to try his luck. "Let's take it, boys!" he yelled, and he led the way up the banks of a protecting ditch. The Texas riflemen gave them perfect cover. Bowie's sudden appearance for the moment paralyzed the enemy. He and his men seized the weapon, then turned it on the fleeing soldiers. When the fog cleared, 100 Mexicans were dead; Bowie had lost one man.

Following this victory, the volunteers wanted to march straight on to attack General Cós's main army in San Antonio. Austin, on Houston's advice, vetoed the idea. This was all the army Texas had; to lose it would be to lose all. Cós was a wily veteran, not to be taken lightly. Plans had to be laid.

Rather than attack, Austin decided on a siege. Jim Bowie,

San Fernando Church and the main plaza of San Antonio

angered by the decision, resigned from the army and left.
But he soon returned to the volunteer force, which he was to
command at the Alamo.

The Convention Meets

For several weeks the army marked time; this particularly
vexed the volunteers from the United States who had come
for adventure; they were bored stiff.

But the Convention, finally meeting at San Felipe in early
November, was anything but inactive. After fierce debate,
the majority of its fifty or so delegates voted against a declaration of independence from Mexico.

Sam Houston, surprisingly, agreed; it was too soon, he
thought, to set up a new republic. The Convention declared
its loyalty to the Mexican Constitution of 1824, thus branding
Santa Anna a usurper. The Texans at this time were fighting
to defend the rights guaranteed them when they settled the
province.

The Convention also named Sam Houston Commander-in-Chief of the Regular Army, and dispatched Austin to the States to raise money and more volunteers. It named a governor, Henry Smith, and a fifteen-member council.

Austin's departure left General Edward Burleson, a veteran Indian fighter and a Houston supporter, in charge of the Texas camp at San Antonio.

For six weeks Burleson did nothing. Reports from spies claimed that General Cós could not get enough food for his horses or his men and that his officers and soldiers were in a state of mutiny. But the volunteers grew restive; they wanted action.

Milam Makes a Move

It was Ben Milam who finally lit the fuse of discontent. Milam had served as a volunteer during Mexico's revolt against Spain, staying on in the Mexican Army until Santa Anna became dictator and he was forced to flee to Texas. Though he called himself "Old Ben," he was only forty-six years old and full of fire.

One day in early December he emerged from Burleson's tent and yelled for attention. "Boys!" he shouted, waving his hat toward Cós's headquarters, "Who'll go with Old Ben into San Antonio?"

The response was overwhelming.

Everybody, it seemed, was eager to go but Burleson. Leaving a small force to guard the camp, Millan took 300 men.

He knew that Cós had divided his troops in half. One body was to defend the town; the other was to maintain as a refuge the old mission-fortress known as the Alamo, half a mile to the east, and across the river.

San Antonio's center consisted of two plazas lying east

December, 1835: Texans capture fort of San Antonio de Bexar.

and west of the San Fernando Church. Both plazas had been strongly fortified with cannon fixed in pits and breastworks thrown up in front of them. Any approach through the main streets would thus be exposed to direct artillery fire. Cós had also posted snipers on the flat roofs of the adobe buildings all over town.

A Feint Works

Milam had to attack the plazas first to get possession of the defending cannon. Without these he could never breach the Alamo's thick walls. His only hope was to try a feint on the Alamo itself to draw the Mexican soldiers away from the plazas. He assigned this operation to Colonel James Neill.

The Texans fixed the rendezvous at an old mill north of town for midnight, December 4th. Milam hoped to sneak two of his columns into some large vacant houses which stood on the edge of the plaza while the Mexicans had their eyes on what they believed to be the main attack against the Alamo.

The feint worked. Before daylight, Milam got his men to cover before the sentinels in the plaza realized what was happening. His strategy now was to take the town, drive the Mexicans into the Alamo, then lay siege to it. Cós would have to live off his meager winter supplies; once shut up in the Alamo, he could be starved out.

The time had come for the Texans to storm the plaza fortifications. On the north sides of these town squares were rows of houses—lined up wall-to-wall. Thus the Texans were able, with crowbars and hatchets and battering rams, to move from one house to another, while still protected from enemy fire by the outside walls. This maneuver gave them a fort in front of the two plazas adjoining the church.

One of the Texans' first conquests was the Veramendi "palace," which had a small courtyard in front. Milam decided to set up trenchwork there. On the second day, as he was directing this operation, he was killed by a rooftop sniper. Lieutenant-Colonel Francis Johnson took command.

On the third day Cós ordered all his men into the Alamo. The next morning, to the surprise of the Texans, he ran up the white flag of surrender above the walls.

What had happened to make victory suddenly so easy?

The battle-hungry volunteers hated to admit it, but Austin, even Burleson, had been proved right. The siege which they advocated would have worked. San Antonio could have been taken without firing a shot. Cós was starved out: the corn was gone, the soldiers had been killing their own mounts for meat; there had been many desertions.

Cós demanded favorable terms of surrender, but he was in no position to bargain. The Texans made him swear never to return to fight above the Rio Grande again. He left in their hands a sizable quantity of cannon (including fourteen at the Alamo, alone) and much-needed stores of side arms and ammunition.

"Matamoros Fever"

The Alamo now became the headquarters for the "volunteer" army, with Francis Johnson in charge. This group was quite separate from the Regular Army, of which Sam Houston had been appointed Commander-in-Chief.

Flushed with victory, Colonel Johnson and his friend, Dr. James Grant, wanted to push the war on into Mexico, there to join forces with the core of Mexican republicans who were against Santa Anna's dictatorship.

Grant specifically proposed mounting an expedition against the Mexican Gulf port of Matamoros, a flourishing and rich harbor city. This idea appealed to the volunteers who wanted action, especially to the New Orleans Greys. Soon after Christmas, Johnson and Grant stripped the Alamo of guns, blankets and ammunition, and set out with two hundred men. Colonel James Fannin, then stationed at Goliad, which was on the way, planned to join them.

Sam Houston and Governor Smith, looked on this "Matamoros Fever" as sheer folly. The Council took the opposite view. The argument raged for a month; finally Houston talked Fannin out of going along, and the campaign stalled. It would have meant leaving Texas wholly unguarded if Santa Anna should invade. This was a real possibility; sooner or later he would try to avenge Cós's defeat.

But nobody thought he could arrive with an army before spring. The winter would make transporting an army bitterly difficult; for one thing there would be no grass on the ground for the horses and mule teams.

Santa Anna meant every word of it when he announced that he was arriving in person to subdue the Texas rebels. One of his advance units encountered the retreating Cós. Santa Anna ordered him to turn around and march back to the Rio Grande, where his main army of about five thousand men was to be assembled by February 12th.

Eleven days later, after a forced march which worked great hardship on his men, he reached the outskirts of San Antonio. Santa Anna was taking no prisoners. He had come to kill. And he caught the squabbling Texans completely unprepared.

Santa Anna planned first to retake San Antonio and the Alamo, then to mop up the rest of the territory. He even threatened that if the United States didn't stop helping the Texans, he would march all the way to Washington.

His presence in their midst would soon bring the Texans to their senses with a jolt.

The Alamo chapel is all that remains of the fortress-mission.

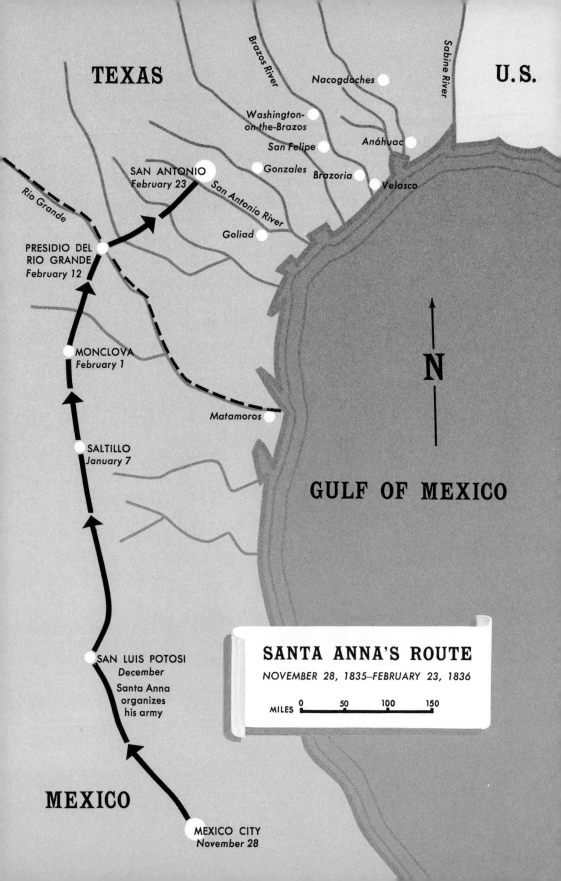

TEXAS

U.S.

Brazos River

Sabine River

Nacogdoches

Washington-
on-the-Brazos

Anáhuac

San Felipe

SAN ANTONIO
February 23

San Antonio River

Gonzales

Brazoria

Velasco

Rio Grande

Goliad

PRESIDIO DEL
RIO GRANDE
February 12

MONCLOVA
February 1

Matamoros

N

SALTILLO
January 7

GULF OF MEXICO

SAN LUIS POTOSI
December

Santa Anna
organizes
his army

SANTA ANNA'S ROUTE

NOVEMBER 28, 1835–FEBRUARY 23, 1836

MILES 0   50   100   150

MEXICO

MEXICO CITY
November 28

2

The Days of Siege

LIKE A magnet, the Alamo drew men to it.

Originally a Franciscan mission, the three-acre compound of stone and adobe buildings was almost as old as San Antonio itself.

But no amount of zeal could bring any change in the Indians of Texas. By 1793 the missions were abandoned, and the long effort ceased. About 1800 the mission San Antonio de Valero became known as the Alamo. It was used as barracks and headquarters by a Spanish troop of Indian fighters, whose home base back in Coahuila was called the Alamo and who gave the same name to their new temporary home. Some insist, however, the name comes from the Spanish words, *los alamos*, for the huge cottonwoods that grew around it.

After 1800 it was used as a fort only from time to time. By 1836 it was in a sad state of disrepair. The sturdiest building was the chapel, though its roof had caved in long ago.

The fortress-mission was a kind of walled rectangular plaza, about the size and dimensions of a football field—150 yards long by 56 yards wide. Within the outside walls on the south and west sides were adobe brick rooms. On the east were similar rooms, two-stories high in the midsection. These had housed the convent of the mission. The church or chapel, which is all people think of today when they think of the Alamo, was set back about fifty feet at the southeast corner, thus having its own little court in front of it. The walls generally were some three feet thick and nine feet in height. The walls of the two-story convent rose as high as twenty feet.

To the north of the chapel were enclosed areas for gardening and storage, and a cattle pen. A gap existed between the south side of the chapel and the south wall of the plaza. The Texans closed this breach by setting up a stockade fence— double rows of stout posts—and filling the spaces between with hard-packed earth to absorb the impact of cannon balls.

A New Arrival

Sam Houston recommended to Bowie and Travis and Neill that they blow up the Alamo and move its cannon into the Anglo settlements. All three leaders stubbornly maintained this would be a mistake. The Alamo, in their view, was the key to the defense of Texas. If Santa Anna got it, they reasoned, he would have the strongest fort in the territory. There he could not only resist attack, he could send out from it forces to conquer the score or so of American settlements one by one.

Early in February, Bowie wrote to Governor Smith underlining the necessity of defending the Alamo: "Colonel Neill and myself have come to the solemn resolution that we will rather die in these ditches than give them up to the enemy."

On the morning of February 8th, another extraordinary character from Tennessee made a dramatic appearance in San Antonio. He was already the most famous frontiersman in the nation, even more of a legend than Jim Bowie. Like

Davy Crockett

Houston, he had been a Congressman from Tennessee. Now fifty years old, he was still ruggedly handsome, lively, cheerful and humorous.

This man was Davy Crockett.

When he was defeated in running for re-election to Congress in 1835, he told the Tennessee voters they could go "roast in hell," and he would go to Texas. Some of his neighbors remarked that it would be all the same.

Crockett and a dozen companions arrived at San Antonio on the same day that Santa Anna's main army reached the Rio Grande, 150 miles below the Alamo.

Houston Heads East

Gradually, all the principal actors in the great drama were coming together. Sam Houston was the only exception. Technically Commander-in-Chief of the Texas armies, he moved out of the Alamo's magic radius. In his disgust with the squabbling between the two rival factions of the interim government, he was biding his time until a new convention scheduled for March 1st could resolve the quarrel and give him full authority.

But there was still a major service to be performed, and he undertook it. Santa Anna's agents were trying to incite the 2,000 Cherokees in East Texas to go over to the Mexican side. Houston asked Governor Smith for a furlough till March 1st and went to Nacogdoches to make a treaty with the Indians.

Surprising News

Davy Crockett's arrival in San Antonio set off a week-long celebration. The Texans knew all about him. The sight of him in his coonskin cap and buckskin breeches, carrying his favorite long rifle, "Old Betsy," was like a tonic, proof that the Americans "back home" cared about the Texas venture. The Alamo men gathered around him to inspect "Old Betsy."

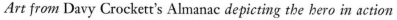

Art from Davy Crockett's Almanac *depicting the hero in action*

The Texans wanted to make Davy a colonel in their army right away. This seemed to be an army in which everybody held rank. "I'll just be a kind of high private," he replied, and added, "Me and my boys heard you were having a little trouble with ole Santy Anny, so we came along to help out in the fight."

The shouting and cheers gave way to speechmaking, for Davy was a celebrated yarn-spinner and orator. He also performed on his fiddle, while a Scot named McGregor accompanied him on the bagpipes.

The celebration was to come to a climax on George Washington's birthday with cockfights, horse races, dances and speeches. Toward midnight the festivities were suddenly interrupted. A scout arrived with a message for Travis and Bowie. Santa Anna, with his main army, unbelievably, was encamped on the Medina River, only a score or so miles away.

The messenger was Captain Juan Seguin, member of a distinguished old Mexican family in San Antonio who had cast his lot with the Texans.

Seguin also reported that had the river not been flooded, preventing Santa Anna from ferrying his artillery across, he would have executed a surprise attack that very night.

To avoid being caught off guard a second time, Travis and Bowie at once posted a sentry on the roof of San Fernando Church.

The View from the Tower

In the dawn light of February 23rd, the young sentry stood shivering in the tower of San Fernando Church. He could see faintly the dun-colored walls of the Alamo lying half a mile to the east beyond a bend in the San Antonio

River. To the south and west the land was flat, dotted with mesquite. To the north low blue hills stretched away in the distance.

Again and again his eyes swept the horizon. Everywhere he looked, the landscape lay wrapped in the stillness of fading night. Somewhere he heard a rooster crow. No sign of life to the south, to the east, to the north.

Then, as he looked once more to the west, the breath went out of him.

The veil of darkness was lifting now. There on the heights, the gathering light revealed hundreds, perhaps thousands of helmets, pennants, banners. These must be—could only be— the Mexican lancers.

For a moment, panic nearly immobilized the youth. Then he seized the bell rope on the church tower and pulled with all his might. The ear-splitting peals brought Travis and Dr. John Sutherland, one of the post's six physicians, from the plaza below, up the rickety wooden stairs two steps at a time.

But the pealing of the bell also served as warning to the Mexican troops to take cover. When Travis and Sutherland looked out from the top of the tower, they saw nothing. Perhaps, they thought, fear and the strain of the long night's waiting had played tricks with the young sentry's senses.

Dr. Sutherland had a horse below; so did his friend John W. Smith. The two of them volunteered to ride out on a scouting foray to the western hills to see for sure. "Keep an eye on us," Sutherland said to Travis. "If we come racing back, then you'll know what to do."

Two Scouts Go Out

A mile and a half out of town, at the top of a gentle rise, the two men reined in their horses. From there they could look down into a hidden valley. They were astonished at what they saw. Below them, the sun flashed on the muskets and lances of soldiers at drill.

Smith and Sutherland wheeled around and headed back to the Alamo. They whipped their ponies to a breakneck speed, praying they had not been observed by the Mexicans. But the road was still slippery from the rain. Halfway home, Dr. Sutherland's mount stumbled and fell, throwing its rider. Smith, who saw the mishap, whirled about. Sutherland's spill had lamed himself but not his horse. Smith got them both up, and on they went.

The two men raced into town as the sentry, who had seen them coming, was again pulling at the bell rope with all his might.

Inside the Alamo

Immediately Travis ordered the Texans into the Alamo. He ought to have had a thousand men to defend that stronghold alone. With a force of only 150 available to him, he knew it would be sheer foolhardiness to try to defend the town of San Antonio as well. The fighting men would have to take refuge in the old fort until help arrived from the Anglo settlements and from Colonel Fannin. The noncombatants would have to flee.

Among those who had gathered at the Alamo was Travis' friend, James Bonham, a fabulous horseman who had been known to ride a hundred miles in less than two days. It was Bonham, therefore, whom Travis had already dispatched to bring Colonel Fannin and his men from Goliad to the Alamo. Bonham was due back at any moment. Surely, Fannin could not be far behind.

Travis left Crockett to handle the withdrawal into the

Alamo (the first and only retreat these men made); then he hastened to the fort to make ready.

Jim Bowie had caught pneumonia following a bad fall from a ramp where he had been placing a cannon in position. He was now seriously ill; but he had his wits about him. He detailed men to round up all the cattle in sight and drive them into the pens next to the chapel. He sent others to raid barns for grain. Within the space of a few hours, thirty beeves went through the gates; eighty sacks of corn were carted, or carried, into the Alamo. Now the defenders were prepared for a long siege. They might have nothing to eat but corn and beef—but at least they weren't going to starve.

Sentries scoured the horizon for some sight of Bonham. Fannin, who had been unwilling to share command with Travis or Bowie or anyone else, had spent the past month working his men at perfecting the little fort at Goliad, indifferent to all pleas to join in uniting the Texas defense. With Santa Anna so close at hand, however, he would have no choice now but to cooperate. No one doubted Bonham would bring word that Fannin had already begun the three-day journey to the Alamo.

"No Quarter"

Santa Anna was losing no time. Shortly after noon, on February 23rd, in resplendent regalia, he rode into San Antonio and took possession of the town, which had already been emptied.

Santa Anna had with him about twenty-five hundred troops. At least as many more were following behind.

When the Mexican General had settled himself in his new headquarters in San Antonio, almost as a matter of routine he sent a message to the Texans in the Alamo, in care of

In full-dress uniform, Santa Anna parades through Mexico City.

Bowie, demanding unconditional surrender. Santa Anna was under the impression that the mere presence of his formidable army would be enough to frighten the Texans into submission.

Bowie, of course, flatly rejected the terms. He did reply, however, that he would be willing to meet Santa Anna for a parley; he saw no harm in that.

Bowie had a lot to lose in fighting. By this time, he and his father-in-law must have owned a million or more acres. He had been notably successful in negotiating with the Mexicans, and saw no reason why he should not first try to solve this problem by the same means.

It angered Travis that, although he shared authority with Bowie, it was to the latter, his long-time rival, that Santa

Anna's message was addressed. Bowie seemed to be, in Santa Anna's eyes, the decision-maker.

Without consulting Bowie or anyone else, Travis quickly ordered a gunner to fire a cannon ball into the air. This was to be the Texan's answer—clear and contemptuous—delivered with gunfire.

Santa Anna hastened to reply in kind. He quickly ran up a red flag on the tower of San Fernando Church. This was significant. The red flag meant "no quarter"—no surrender, no prisoners taken, only death.

War of Nerves

But Santa Anna, though impetuous, could also be patient when he chose. His fieldpieces, his artillery, were for the most part still on the way. Other battalions were also en route. After their brutally long forced march across the semi-desert his exhausted men were badly in need of a respite.

He would bide his time. He contented himself now with posting guards around the Alamo to close retreat exits and with stationing units on the roads to intercept any troops who might be coming to the assistance of the garrison.

The Mexican General was a past master of the war of nerves; indeed, he had built his entire military career on terrorism. While he waited and watched, he ordered his regimental bands to blare away night after night, from dusk to dawn. The object of this strategy was to keep the Texans from their sleep and so wear down their resistance. It succeeded all too well.

But there were other developments calculated to depress the Texans. Just at dusk, on the very first day of the siege, a weary horseman on a foam-flecked mount dashed through the gates with the enemy in close pursuit.

It was Jim Bonham. He had come to report on his interview with Colonel Fannin. The news was not good; Fannin was adamant. He still saw no reason why he should leave Goliad. In fact he had refused to budge.

There was only one sustaining note of hope. At the time of Bonham's interview a few days before, Santa Anna had not yet reached San Antonio. The situation, therefore, did not appear to be critical. Travis was convinced that as soon as Fannin learned how things really stood, he would head for the Alamo in a hurry.

Bonham also brought word of possible aid from another source. On his way back, he had crossed paths with Sutherland and Smith, who were carrying the word to the colonies concerning Santa Anna's surprise arrival. From them he learned that the new Texas Convention was scheduled to meet on March 1st at Washington-on-the-Brazos.

If the tiny garrison of the Alamo could manage to hold out through the intervening week, then surely support would not be long in coming from the Convention.

President-General Santa Anna's silver-plated bridle and spurs

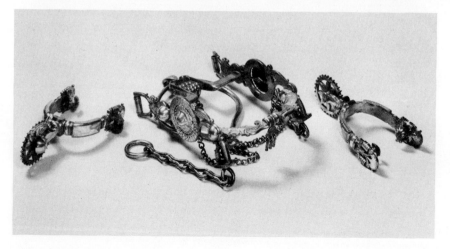

A factor working in their favor was that Santa Anna seemed to be in no hurry. He even took time out to fall in love. It happened this way: he needed lumber to build new bridges over the river, since the only one in existence was insufficient for his needs. While he was requisitioning wood-frame houses to be demolished for bridge-building, he met, in one of them, a beautiful señorita, Melchora Barrera.

Santa Anna was already married. But to satisfy the girl's mother, he arranged a mock wedding ceremony, performed by one of his lieutenants disguised as a priest. The mother gave her blessing to the honeymoon and yielded her house for timber.

All the Mexicans were not idling, however. Santa Anna's leading strategist, a brilliant Spaniard named Castrillón, became disgusted with his chief's behavior. He did his best to organize the siege and surround the Alamo with a series of manned entrenchments. He cut off irrigation ditches from the river, but the Texans had already dug a well within the walls, so that didn't bother them.

These maneuvers exposed the Mexican soldiers to the long rifles of the Texans, who gave the first demonstration of their marksmanship. Davy Crockett awed the Mexicans by picking off one of them who was standing at a bend in the river and who was under the impression that he was safe because he was a great distance away.

Few among the Texans were experienced in soldiering; but their frontier way of life, in which food so often depended on their skill in bagging game, stood them in good stead. And whether they knew it or not, they had the superior rifles; these were accurate up to a distance of two hundred yards. But the Mexican *escopetas*, bought from England as remainders after the Battle of Waterloo, reached effectively only up to about seventy yards.

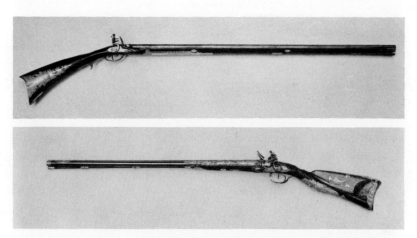

Top: A Kentucky rifle. Bottom: A presentation flintlock fowling piece made for Napoleon I (Metropolitan Museum of Art)

The Texans held their cannon fire. Ammunition was valuable, and if help did not come from Fannin the stockpile would soon be low.

On that first day, not a single Texan was killed. But that night, under cover of darkness, the Mexicans were busy setting up their battery positions 400 yards west of the Alamo. In the morning, the cannonading would start in earnest.

Travis Writes a "Message to the World"

On the evening of Feburary 24th, Travis sat alone at a table in his bare adobe room—a room which had once been a monk's cell—and wrote out his first "message to the world," which he would dispatch the next day.

Few documents in American history match the spirit or fervor of his famous statement. He meant it to rouse the American nation, just as the brief appeals of the day before, carried out by Smith and Sutherland, were meant to spur the citizens of Gonzales and Goliad and other Texas towns to action.

Commandancy of the Alamo
Bexar, F'by 24th, 1836

To the people of Texas & All Americans in the World:

Fellow Citizens and Compatriots—I am besieged by a thousand or more of the Mexicans under Santa Anna. I have sustained a continual bombardment and cannonade for 24 hours and have not lost a man. The enemy has demanded a surrender at discretion, otherwise, the garrison are to be put to the sword, if the fort is taken. I have answered the demand with a cannon shot, and our flag still waves proudly from the walls. *I shall never surrender or retreat.* Then I call upon you in the name of Liberty, of patriotism, and everything dear to the American character, to come to our aid with all dispatch. The enemy is receiving reinforcements daily and will no doubt increase to three or four thousand in four or five days. If this call is neglected, I am determined to sustain myself as long as possible and die like a soldier who never forgets what is due to his own honor and that of his country: VICTORY OR DEATH.

William Barret Travis
LT. COL. COMDT.

Torchbearers

On the third day, Santa Anna decided that the time had come to close in. About three hundred yards directly south of the main gate, the Mexicans set up a battery of cannon. Travis, looking out from the walls of the Alamo, saw something that filled him with alarm. A number of straw huts still dotted the area between the Alamo and the new artillery position. The Texans had neglected to destroy them. These huts would afford excellent cover to Mexicans getting ready to cross the river under the protection of cannon fire.

On the night before, the defenders had gone out of the fort on a sortie to get wood for campfires and scaffoldings from the huts on the southeast side. The same operation could be repeated to the south—except for one thing. Travis could not afford to wait for nightfall. Volunteers must be dispatched at once—even though it meant going out in broad daylight to get rid of the remaining shelters. Mustering out the defenders, he called for two men; dozens stepped forward. Only two, he repeated, and chose Charles Despallier and Robert Brown, both youngsters.

Artillery and rifle fire—the rifles were under Davy Crockett's command—would cover them.

Out they dashed. The first salvo burst from the Alamo. The Mexicans replied. A fierce gun duel ensued. While bullets and cannon balls whizzed around them, Despallier and Brown zigzagged from hut to hut, putting torch to timber and straw. Then they ran back to the Alamo, at top speed, leaving behind them a raging inferno.

A roar of relief greeted them as they reached the walls unscathed. The barrage, meant only as a protection for their feat, had triggered a full-scale battle, which the Texans won. The Mexicans had been forced to retreat; the Alamo cannon had proved their effectiveness.

Travis, immensely proud of his young men, sent off a letter to Houston describing their courageous exploit. "But," he added, "do send help at once. We are besieged."

A Secret Trail

Other Texans went out that night and succeeding nights on sorties to burn other huts. It was dangerous work, for it meant eluding not only the prowling Mexican patrols, but the larger detachments which were now digging themselves in, moving closer and closer to the Alamo walls.

Each morning revealed an increasingly bleak prospect to

the forlorn sentinels who climbed the ramps to look eastward for the arrival of aid. On every side, daylight revealed greater encroachment by the Mexicans.

The Alamo was not so hermetically sealed as Santa Anna fancied. Possibilities for communication with the outside world still existed. Unknown to him, a secret trail enabled couriers to move in and out. All in all, some twenty of them slipped through at various times with their messages. Two of them, Jim Bonham and John W. Smith, got back in—Bonham to stay and Smith to carry out the last verified reports.

Santa Anna knew nothing of this trail until the tenth day of the siege.

On February 27th the weather turned bad. A bitter wind whistled in from the north to chill the sleepless Texans. Santa Anna's bands still blared: the defenders' nerves were becoming frayed with fatigue; tempers grew short. Davy Crockett did his best to enliven his companions with his jokes and by playing his fiddle, but it was uphill work. Bowie, increasingly ill, was now confined to his bed. He was being cared for by some of the Mexican women who had come in with Juan Seguin's company, and by Susannah Dickinson, eighteen-year-old wife of the Texan artillery chief, Almeron Dickinson.

The hours dragged on. Travis estimated that he must have dispatched a dozen couriers. But no word had come back from any of them. Was it possible that none had gotten through? The lack of news from the outside world preyed on his mind. It also depressed the men. He decided to try again. The man best qualified was the one Travis wanted most to have at his side in this bleak hour—Jim Bonham. But if anybody could perform the mission, Bonham could. In addition to being a great horseman, he was eloquent and per-

Mrs. Susannah Dickinson,
long after the Alamo massacre

suasive. Travis instructed him to offer Fannin anything to get him to come, to point out that the Mexican Army was getting reinforcements daily, while the Texans at the Alamo were outnumbered about fifty to one! While the two were laying plans for the expedition, one thing puzzled them— how were they to identify Bonham as he approached the Alamo? Then Travis had an idea. "Tie a white handerchief around your hat," he said. "I'll have men watching from the walls. When we see you we'll be ready with the gates." Travis shook his hand, then climbed a ramp to watch his closest friend ride away. He knew that his own fate and the fate of all his men rode with Bonham.

Two days later, on February 29th, Travis saw his situation was getting desperate. He called for two volunteer couriers.

No one came forward. To volunteer to go now might look like cowardice. Travis had to choose. So he sent out Juan Seguin and Antonio Arocha. If they got caught, their Spanish might help them to escape. Their mission was to go to Gonzales and on to the Texas Convention, scheduled to meet next day at Washington-on-the-Brazos, 150 miles away.

Travis was sparing his men, conserving his ammunition. He also kept from his officers his growing sense of hopelessness. He and they strained their ears to catch the hoofbeats of Fannin's troops; all they heard was Mexican gunfire, doubly loud now that the Texans had silenced theirs.

At Goliad and Gonzales

There was no need now to wait for Fannin, although he had at last made up his mind. At dusk on February 28th he had set out for the Alamo with 400 men.

A few miles beyond his fort, three supply wagons broke down. While the troops were encamped that night, many of the oxen, turned loose to feed, escaped. Next morning Fannin called a council of his officers. Should they proceed without artillery and with scant supplies? While they were debating, Colonel Johnson, leader of the ill-fated expedition to Matamoros, rode furiously into camp. He had barely escaped capture at the hands of another wing of Santa Anna's army.

This force consisted of 1,000 men under the command of General José Urrea. Urrea, gasped Johnson breathlessly, was at this moment only two days' march from Goliad.

That settled it. Fannin felt justified in not abandoning Fort Defiance, as he had named the stronghold. His troops came back across the river, hauling and pushing the wagons themselves. Fannin had written off the Alamo; now he had to prepare his own line of defense.

At Gonzales, a little band of 32 men (some were mere boys) had been waiting for Fannin since February 25th. They had planned to join his men en route to the Alamo. But then Dr. Sutherland and John Smith brought their news; it was quickly relayed to the surrounding settlements.

By February 29th, the men at Gonzales, including every able-bodied male in the area, knowing that Fannin was definitely stalled, embarked on a heroic act. They were quite aware that the bare handful of volunteers that they could muster had no chance of tipping the scales at the Alamo. But they did feel a strong sense of duty to Travis and the others; and they had their self-respect. John W. Smith told them he knew how to guide them into the fort. The men, ranging

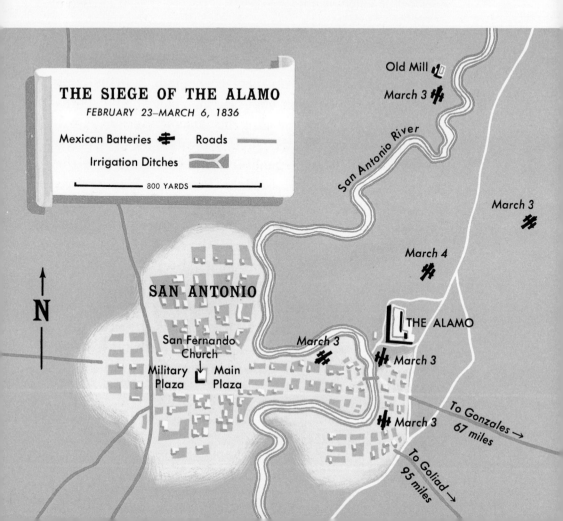

THE SIEGE OF THE ALAMO

FEBRUARY 23–MARCH 6, 1836

Mexican Batteries Roads

Irrigation Ditches

800 YARDS

Old Mill

March 3

San Antonio River

March 3

March 4

SAN ANTONIO

THE ALAMO

San Fernando Church

March 3

Military Plaza Main Plaza

March 3

N

March 3

To Gonzales → 67 miles

To Goliad → 95 miles

in age from fifteen to forty-eight, stepped forward. One youngster, hesitating, asked an older man, "How do we know we can ever get out?" The man replied, "Hell, son, don't worry about that. We ain't even got in it yet." Every one of them knew in his heart that he had made a decision to die.

Sometime early in the morning of March 1st they appeared along the trail outside the dun-colored walls. The Texans, thinking at first that these were the advance guard of Fannin's four or five hundred men, greeted them with cheers and shouts. A stunned silence followed. When they learned the truth, the Texans gave the Gonzales men—who had already sacrificed greatly to join the fight—an even heartier welcome; they brought out sides of their precious beef and held a barbecue celebration.

The Drawn Line

Perhaps the most dramatic of all entries into the Alamo was the return of Jim Bonham, about eleven o'clock on the morning of March 3rd. Barely eluding the pursuing Mexican patrol, he whipped his sweat-lathered pony through the open gates, waving his hat with the handkerchief tied around it to the sentries on the wall. He brought Travis the long-awaited news of Fannin.

Fannin had tried to persuade Bonham not to go back to certain death. "We need you here," he said, "and when we win you can serve Texas a long time." Bonham's reply was not recorded.

Now Travis had to break the bad news to the men. It was the tenth day of the siege. There was a lull in the firing in the late afternoon (the Mexicans were celebrating the arrival of more troops). Travis called for files on parade in the courtyard.

Jim Bowie was carried out on his cot into the late afternoon sunlight.

For a few moments, Travis was unable to speak. Then he mastered his emotion. "I know," he began, "I have promised you that help would come. Well, I have deceived you." He, in turn, had been deceived, he added, by the promises of others. Every report from the Texas Council had assured him that recruits from the colonies would come to their aid.

Only now, today, had it become crystal clear that the promised support would never get here in time. Travis admitted that he could no longer hold out any hope, not only of receiving any assistance, but even of survival. "Our fate is sealed," he said, his voice steady. "Within a very few days —perhaps a very few hours—we must all be in eternity. This is our destiny and we cannot avoid it. This is our certain doom."

The crimson sunset of late Texas winter washed the horizon as the leader and his men stood facing each other. Then, in a gesture of generosity, Travis exonerated the leaders of Texas, the government, the Convention, Fannin, and others for misleading them all and putting them in this position. He added, "We must sell our lives as dearly as possible." Every man, he pointed out, had a choice. Escape was still possible; hadn't twenty couriers already slipped through the Mexican lines? "For myself," Travis finished, "I will fight as long as there is a breath in my body."

He drew a line with his sword across the ground in front of the troops. "I want every man who is determined to stay here with me and die," he said, "to cross this line." In a solid row the men stepped forward. There were, however, two exceptions. One was Jim Bowie. He had to wait a bit for four men to come and lift him over the line in his cot.

The other was a soldier of fortune, a refugee from France,

Travis asks for the allegiance—and the lives—of his valiant men.

named Moses Rose. A mercenary, he had come to the New World to fight in it, not to save it. He alone chose to escape. The men understood; he was here for reasons of his own. He did not share their feeling for this land.

Rose made his escape and lived to tell the tale. His testimony is the only evidence existing that documents Travis' speech and his drawing of the line. Some historians regard this evidence as insufficient. But others believe that the fact that this account is in a way derogatory to Rose himself is convincing proof that he was telling the truth.

One other Texan left the Alamo that night on a mission. He was John W. Smith, the great courier. Travis sent him with a final desperate plea to the Texas Convention then in assembly. Possibly a secondary motive was to let the men send out last letters to their kin. Travis had one or two messages he wanted to send himself. On a piece of wrapping paper that is still preserved, he quickly scribbled this note to a friend who was looking after his six-year-old son (the boy had been brought west to his father in 1835):

Take care of my little boy. If the country should be saved, I may make him a splendid fortune; but if the country should be lost—he will have nothing but the proud recollection that he is the son of a man who died for his country.

The men of the garrison accepted calmly their inevitable fate. There were now 187 of them. Nineteen were from England and Europe; a scattering was from the northern states; 32 were from Tennessee, with other southern states contributing about a dozen each. Nine or ten were of Mexican descent, the only ones who had been born and raised in Texas. In common comradeship, they were all resigned to die together in the cause of freedom.

Meanwhile, at Washington-on-the-Brazos, unmindful of their plight, the Convention moved briskly forward with its agenda. In the few days since the delegates had assembled, it had created a new Texas government, renamed Sam Houston Commander-in-Chief of its Army, and at long last issued a Declaration of Independence. Of all this the men at the Alamo knew nothing, even though they were the ones who were making it possible through their resistance.

Day of Decision

March 5th was to have been the day. Bitter, bleak weather blew in, hampering the attack.

For Santa Anna, it was a day when he had to decide. Some of his generals, including Castrillón, still wanted to delay the all-out assault until heavier cannon arrived from Saltillo.

The staff knew that if the Alamo walls were not decisively breached, the Mexican foot soldiers would be sacrificed in appalling numbers. All that the Mexican light artillery had been able to achieve so far was a small break in the northeast bastion of the Alamo, too meager to allow troops to pour through.

That Saturday afternoon Santa Anna stilled his guns and summoned his officers. The hour had come; the all-out blow must be struck. He could no longer prolong the siege.

Santa Anna's instructions were precise.

At four the next morning, in light just sufficient for scaling the Alamo walls yet too dim to reveal the plan of the attack, the infantry, carrying ladders, would charge the fort from all four sides. The cavalry would back up the infantry, to intercept escaping Texans—and also to halt any retreat of Mexican foot soldiers.

Santa Anna had about five thousand men against the 187 beleaguered Texans. The General was curiously considerate of his enemies. After nights of nonstop serenading by his military bands, and days thunderous with cannon fire, he would let the weary defenders sleep.

It would take a while for them to wake. By the time they did, his men would already be scaling the walls. They had twenty-eight ladders—seven for each of the four points of attack.

General Cós, with 700 men, would strike from the Mexican camp opposite the northwest corner of the Alamo; General Duque, with the same number, would attack from the northeast; General Romero would lead 300 men from the east camp; and General Morales, assigned to attack the Texans' weakest point, would move up from the south side with about 100 men. General Santa Anna took charge of the reserves, gathered on the north-side camp; he could replace

Cós if the latter fell. Concentrating on the break in the north wall, Santa Anna had moved his cannon on that side up to a position within two hundred yards of the breach.

A Lull

Huddled at their posts against the freezing wind, the Texans slept. We know the names of the leaders: Bowie, Crockett, Travis. But who were the others waiting there that night of destiny? There was young James Rose, nephew of President James Madison. There were three young brothers from Liberty, Texas: Edward, George and James Taylor. There was the Alamo surgeon Amos Pollard, from New York, who had been caring for Jim Bowie. There was Almeron Dickinson from Tennessee, whose wife and fifteen-month-old daughter were sheltered in the chapel sacristy below the cannon he operated on the chapel roof. There was Johnnie Kellogg, nineteen and young husband of a Gonzales girl he had stolen away from her middle-aged mate. The former husband was there, too, also with the Gonzales group. There was young William Cloud from Kentucky, who had written his mother a letter on Christmas Day telling her that "Texas is where things are happening." There was William Garnett, a wandering Baptist preacher. There was William King, fifteen years old, from Gonzales; he insisted on taking the place of his father with the Gonzales men, for there were eight other children for King Senior to care for.

These were some of the men who stood ready, each to play his part, on that historic day.

Travis wondered at the lull. Outside the walls three sentries stood guard; one man tended the fires within—fires for warmth, for hungry men on duty—for the red-hot pokers that would blaze off the cannon touch-holes.

The First Wave

Three startling, consecutive sounds lifted the sleep-drugged Texans to their feet. A bugle blast sounded from Santa Anna's northern battery, by his instructions. It was picked up and echoed by bugles from camps on each side of the fort. This was the signal for the charge. The bugles' piercing clarity was followed by what seemed at first a thousand drums in muted beating; but this was, in fact, the pounding of thousands of feet as the Mexican infantry dashed over the hard earth, eager to find in the shelter of the Alamo walls protection from the Texas cannon.

Except for Jim Bonham's three eight-pounders on the east wall of the chapel, none of the defenders' cannon could be either pivoted or aimed downward.

The third sound that roused the Texans from their sleep proved the most blood-curdling of all. This was the sound of

After a prolonged siege, Santa Anna's troops storm the Alamo.

the massed bands playing Santa Anna's own theme-song, the famous Moorish battle call of "no quarter," the *Degüello*. Santa Anna, in charge of the reserves, had these regimental bands beside him. It was daybreak of Sunday morning, March 6, 1836. The chiming of the church bells of San Fernando summoning worshipers to Mass this morning would go unheard. Three sentries had been posted outside the walls to warn of the Mexican advance. This time they gave no outcry: they must have been bayoneted almost at once. Travis himself gave the first alarm. Dashing from his room to the breached northeastern wall, his chosen post, he yelled to the men. "Come on, boys! The Mexicans are upon us. Don't surrender. Let's give 'em hell!"

A faint moon still shone in the lightening sky. Travis, with rifle and sword, followed by his slave boy Joe, raced to his station beside the twelve-pounder mounted on a platform. Davy Crockett with his twelve "Tennessee boys" manned the stockade that ran from the chapel westward to the south wall. Jim Bonham, with Almeron Dickinson and Gregorio Esparza, whose brother had joined Santa Anna's army, took charge of the cannon atop the chapel. These guns could fire out over the walls in three directions. Jim Bowie, helplessly ill on his cot, had been moved into the chapel sacristy. Earlier, Davy Crockett had put a brace of loaded pistols into his hands. Jim also had beside him his celebrated bowie knife.

The Texans repulsed the first assault with comparative ease, inflicting terrible carnage. Santa Anna could not yet use his artillery from behind the lines, lest it cut down Mexicans as well as Texans. But the Texas cannon took a powerful toll. One Mexican corporal, in a later report, said that he counted forty of his compatriots who fell dead around him in the first attack.

The superlative marksmanship of the Texans caused so

many casualties at the outset that the defenders got an un-
expected respite. The Mexican Generals called for a retreat
to regroup their decimated units before attempting a second
assault. One repulse did not assure victory, but the Texans,
for the moment at least, were elated. Their success gave them
confidence that they could fight off the next attack. Sentries
scanned the horizon anxiously; help might come at any
moment. To judge by the moans and the groaning below
their walls, the Mexicans had taken a terrible punishment.
They had shown extraordinary bravery that first charge but
bravery had its limits. Some of the units had lost half their
complement.

The Mexican officers were greatly concerned. They dared
not delay the second assault too long. They knew, and the
men were beginning to realize, that the second assault, like
the first, would be suicidal. Nevertheless, Santa Anna decided
to try it.

The Second Wave

Crowbars, axes, ladders were once more assembled; again
the bugles sounded; the second assault surged forth. But no
scaling ladder could stay in place long enough for the attackers to gain a foothold. As soon as the head of a Mexican
appeared over the wall, the Texas rifles drew a bead on him;
down he would go, the ladder going too.

Travis' cannon had a clear line of fire on the charge against
the north wall. As in the first charge when the Mexicans
retreated in such confusion that they trampled their leader,
General Duque, underfoot, the big guns broke it up. Once
more, the columns coming from the east and west turned and
fled. For a moment it looked as though the southern column
on Crockett's side was going to make it. They did get a ladder

Hordes of Mexican soldiers scale the walls during the assault.

in place. But not for long. Again withering cannon and rifle fire repulsed them. The Mexican Generals had to call a halt.

They had to plan a new maneuver in a hurry. Hundreds of their men lay dead or dying. The nerves of the others were at breaking point. The plan was this: the Mexicans were again to storm the Alamo from all four sides, but this time there would be a difference; the attacks on three sides would be feints. The east and west columns were to break suddenly and hasten to join the northern column before the Texans could shift their defenses. The southern attack was to veer to the west to capture the most important Texas cannon.

Death at the North Wall

Again the Mexican bugler, José Gonzales, sounded the signal for the attack. *"Adelante!"* the Mexican Generals shouted to their men. The remaining ladders were reassigned. This time Santa Anna threw in his reserves.

Under the new plan so many men would be massed before the breached north wall that the sheer weight of numbers would force them through the opening, even if they had to climb over the bodies of their comrades.

And so it worked out.

Meanwhile, the south column, led by General Morales, suddenly veered to the west as planned. This time they got ladders up and swarmed over. They were able to seize the Texans' principal defense gun, the eighteen-pounder on a platform near the southwest corner. Others poured after the first attackers. Once inside, the odds in manpower would assure victory.

Travis, according to the report of his slave boy Joe, still manned the north cannon. He was hit, fell, got up. He had been shot through the head, although Joe reported that he drew his sword and with his last ounce of strength cut down a Mexican officer, who died with him.

With the cannon silenced, the floodgate was opened; the Mexicans streamed through the northern breach and through the south gate, now controlled by Morales' men. The Mexican soldiers were cautious now. They dropped to their knees to take aim, or fired from sheltered positions behind remaining fragments of the wall. The foes moved at point-blank range, turning the struggle into hand-to-hand combat, bayonet or sword against knife or tomahawk. Since the Texans no longer had time or space in which to load their rifles, they reversed them and used the butts as clubs.

A few Texans still manned one or two cannon stations. They pulled their guns around to blast away at the enemy in the courtyard; but the Mexican riflemen picked them off in a hurry. Slowly, foot by foot, the defenders withdrew from the plaza. All they could do now was to try to find shelter in their barrack rooms or in the chapel. They barricaded the doors and the few windows with earth packed between hides, creating walls shoulder-high to allow shooting over them. But it availed them nothing. The Mexicans, recklessly piling up corpses, battered them in or in some cases turned the captured Texas cannon on them to blast them—and the men behind them—to bits. Men with bayonets invaded the rooms and finished the job. They fought in a fury, their comrades lying dead about them in fearful numbers.

Two Mexican officers, seeing several Texan flags waving from atop the barracks and the chapel, set out to pull them down and to raise Santa Anna's emblem. They succeeded, but both were shot in the attempt.

Davy Crockett died outdoors, as he would have wished. "I hate to be hemmed in," he always said. He was found beside the stockade wall which had been assigned to him and his "Tennessee boys" to defend. He was surrounded by enemy corpses. Some accounts set the number as high as nineteen. In any event, "Kwocky" as the Mexicans called him, gave a good account of himself. He died fighting against great odds.

The Last Refuge

The Texans found their last refuge in the chapel. Here, in a room on the north, they kept their store of powder. In the early days of the siege, they had sworn a solemn pact that the last man able to so would touch off the magazine and blow everything and everybody to kingdom come.

Major Robert Evans now decided that the moment had arrived. He dashed across the chapel, his arm raised to hurl the torch. Just as he neared the open powder bin, a Mexican bullet cut him down.

Mrs. Dickinson, in a room on the chapel's south side, had three successive shocks. Young Galba Fuqua, a sixteen-year-old from Gonzales, raced to her side to tell her something. His jaw was shattered. Holding it up with both hands, he tried to make her understand, but she could not tell what he was trying to say. He gave her a last look and went back to the cannon-side to die. Her husband had raced in earlier to exclaim: "Great God, Sue, the Mexicans are inside the walls!" Kissing her in farewell, he added, "If they spare you, save our child." And at the very end gunner Jacob Walker, working the chapel cannon with Bonham and Dickinson, rushed to her side. He pleaded for his life with the Mexican soldiers; he had four children to look after in Nacogdoches. They ran him through, then tossed his body on their bayonets, as Mrs. Dickinson reported, "like a bale of hay."

They did the same when they found Jim Bowie, ghost-white, on his cot in the chapel sacristy. They walked out, reported one Mexican woman who tried to shield Bowie, with blood streaming from their arms to their ankles.

General Santa Anna arrived and wanted to be shown the bodies of three men: Travis, Bowie and Crockett. The last Texans to die, according to the report of Ramón Martinez Caro, Santa Anna's personal secretary, were five men who hoped to escape notice by hiding under mattresses. They were found and brought before the Mexican General. At sight of captives left alive, he cursed and turned away. Castrillón tried to intervene in their behalf, but the firing squad did the job. In this war, as Santa Anna had said, there would be no prisoners. Five others had tried to escape by leaping over the walls during the battle; but all had been intercepted by Santa Anna's cavalry and shot.

The victory was complete, not a single Texan defender was left alive.

During the battle Davy Crockett wields "Old Betsy" like a club.

But the cost to the victors was appalling. The Mexican
dead and wounded numbered between 1,000 and 1,500. The
latter figure was the estimate of the neutral mayor of San
Antonio, Francisco Ruiz, who had the job of giving Christian
burial to the Mexican dead. The figure was later confirmed
by Caro. As Colonel Juan Almonte said to his commander,
"Another victory like this one and it will be the death of us!"

Santa Anna had funeral pyres built up to burn the 187
Texas dead.

The Alamo itself was now a battered ruin. But in the past
thirteen days it had become a deathless symbol of the dura-
bility of freedom, one that would be remembered forever.

CHRONOLOGY

1803. Louisiana Purchase. The United States pays France $15 million for Lousiana territory in the west central part of the country. As part of this tract, the United States claims Texas as far as the Rio Grande.

1819. The United States makes treaty with Spain giving up all claim to Texas. In return, Spain gives up Florida. Texas is now a part of Mexico and a Spanish possession.

1821. Mexico wins its independence from Spain.

Stephen F. Austin obtains a land grant from the Mexican Government and establishes a colony of 300 Anglo-Americans on the Lower Brazos River. In 1823 Austin is authorized to create a citizens' army to administer justice and keep the peace.

1824. The Mexican Government sets up a constitutional republic, turning provinces into states.

1825. On March 24th, the Mexican state of Coahuila and Texas enacts a colonization law: each family is to pay $30 for 4,428 acres of land; settlers are to pay no taxes or duties for ten years.

1829. The state of Coahuila and Texas is divided into three departments by Mexican Government: Saltillo, Monclova and Texas.

1830. Texas' population is now more than 20,000, of whom over 15,000 are Americans. On April 6th, Mexico, distrustful of the flood of immigrants, prohibits further colonization in its border states and importation of slaves, and starts to collect customs duties and taxes from the colonists.

1831. To enforce the laws of 1830, Mexico stations troops throughout Texas. General Manuel Mier y Terán abolishes the town council at Liberty and shuts down all Texas ports except the most important one, Anáhuac, on Galveston Bay.

1832, MAY. A Mexican garrison of 300 men is sent to Anáhuac. In jest, William B. Travis tells the garrison's commanding officer, Captain John Davis Bradburn, that 100 armed colonists are marching on the port. Furious, Bradburn jails Travis and one of his companions, Patrick Jack, and prepares to send them to Veracruz for military trial. Angered at this cavalier action, a group of Texans dash to Brazoria, a small settlement 100 miles west, to fetch a cannon. On June 25th, while transporting the cannon by boat, the Texans launch a diversionary attack at Fort Velasco, defeating 150 Mexican soldiers under Colonel Francisco Ugartechea. This is called the First Battle of Anáhuac. Before the schooner arrives at Anáhuac, Colonel José de las Piedras, senior officer in charge of the Mexicans, relieves Bradburn of his command and frees Travis and Jack. The cannon is never used.

1833. Mexico stops collection of duties.

In April, Austin goes to Mexico City with a petition for Texas statehood. It is declined. In October, defying the Mexican Government, Austin writes an open letter to the Mexicans at San Antonio, urging them to support the Anglo-Americans in setting up a state government in Texas.

1834, JANUARY. As a result of his letter, Austin is captured and imprisoned in Mexico City.

APRIL 24. Antonio López de Santa Anna becomes President of Mexico. In May, Santa Anna overthrows the Mexican Constitution of 1824, abolishes the national Congress and state legislatures. Subsequently, the customs laws and taxes are reinstituted.

1835, JANUARY. Mexico again sends troops to Anáhuac to enforce collection of duties. The commander, Captain Antonio Tenorio, orders the arrest of two of Travis' friends for not declaring goods for taxation. In a meeting at San Felipe, Texans led by Travis vote to drive Santa Anna's soldiers and tax collectors out of Anáhuac.

JUNE 30. Travis marches on Anáhuac with 25 men and routs Tenorio's troops.

In August, fearing rebellion, Santa Anna dispatches a force of 500 to San Antonio under command of General Martín Perfecto de Cós. Cós's orders are to arrest Travis and several other leaders.

SEPTEMBER 1. Austin, released from imprisonment, returns to Texas. At Brazoria, he calls for Texans to fight for their constitutional rights and form a provisional government.

OCTOBER 2. Austin, with an army of volunteers, expels 200 Mexicans from Gonzales, 67 miles east of San Antonio. On October 10th, Fort Goliad is seized by a Texas unit under Ben Milam. In the United States, recruitment begins for the Texas cause. One hundred men are enlisted in New Orleans, and on October 20th James Bonham forms a Texas volunteer unit in Mobile, Alabama.

OCTOBER 26. Colonel James Bowie and Colonel James W. Fannin make camp with a force of 100 Texans at Mission Concepción below San Antonio. The next day they defeat 200 of Cós's men nearby.

NOVEMBER 2. In a convention at San Felipe, Texans organize a

CÓS
700 men

DUQUE
700 men

SANTA
ANNA
reserves and
military bands

Breached wall

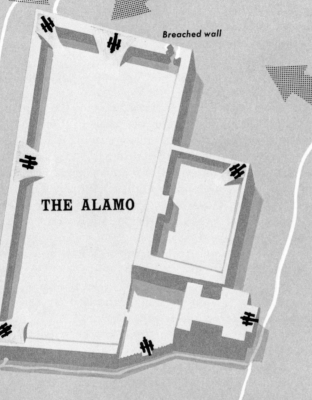

THE ALAMO

ROMERO
300 men

N

MORALES
100 men

THE STORMING OF THE ALAMO
DAWN, MARCH 6, 1836

MEXICAN FORCES   *IRRIGATION DITCHES*

provisional government, naming a governor, Henry Smith, and appointing Sam Houston Commander-in-Chief of the Regular Army. Austin is sent to the United States to solicit funds and assistance for the Texan cause. On November 7th, the Congress proclaims that Texans are fighting to defend the Mexican Constitution of 1824.

NOVEMBER 28. Santa Anna, determined to put down the insurrection, marches for Texas with a force of 5,000 men.

DECEMBER 5. Three hundred volunteers commanded by Ben Milam attack Cós's force at San Antonio. The next day Milam is killed, and Lieutenant-Colonel Francis Johnson takes command.

DECEMBER 10. Cós orders his badly battered troops to retire behind the Rio Grande. The Alamo is now in the hands of the Texans.

1836, JANUARY 19. A handful of recruits under Jim Bowie hastens to the Alamo. Two weeks later, Travis arrives with 30 more men.

FEBRUARY 2. Bowie writes to Governor Smith, appealing for support in holding San Antonio.

FEBRUARY 8. Davy Crockett gallops into San Antonio. His arrival sets off a week-long celebration. Fannin, in command of the fort at Goliad, promises his support.

FEBRUARY 14. The threat to Texas is obviously growing every day. Bowie and Travis agree to divide command of the Alamo between them, but consult each other on major decisions. On February 16th, Santa Anna's forces cross the Rio Grande into Texas. A few days later Travis orders James Bonham to ride for Goliad and appeal to Fannin for help.

FEBRUARY 23, 7 A.M. Anticipating an attack by the Texans, Santa Anna orders his forces to stop at the Alazan Creek. San Antonio is less than two miles away. Just after noon the Mexicans swarm into San Antonio and close in on the Alamo; the siege has begun. Dr. John Sutherland and John W. Smith dash from the fort to alert the colonies of Santa Anna's arrival. At dusk Bonham returns to the Alamo with the news that Fannin will not leave Goliad.

FEBRUARY 24. Bowie, greatly weakened from illness, turns his command over to Travis. In the afternoon, the Mexicans open fire, hammering the fort with a five-inch howitzer and two nine-pounders. Sutherland and Smith are now in Gonzales. That night Travis drafts an appeal to the Convention at Washington-on-the-Brazos, calling upon his fellow Texans "in the name of Liberty, of patriotism, and everything dear to the American character, to come to our aid with all dispatch."

FEBRUARY 25, 10 A.M. The Texans repulse a Mexican attack with devastating cannon and rifle fire. Charles Despallier and Robert

Brown break out of the Alamo and set fire to shacks and huts destroying possible shelter for the advancing enemy. In the evening, the Alamo is pounded by two new Mexican batteries across the river to the south and southwest.

FEBRUARY 26. At dawn, a Mexican cavalry detachment striking toward the rear of the Alamo is driven off by the defenders. During the day, under constant battering from eight Mexican guns, the Texans work furiously to reinforce the fort's walls with earthworks.

FEBRUARY 27. Bonham again rides for Goliad with another appeal to Fannin.

FEBRUARY 28. At dusk, Fannin—though Bonham has not yet arrived at Goliad—starts for the Alamo with 400 men. A few miles from the fort three of his supply wagons break down, and his troops vote to make camp for the night.

FEBRUARY 29. Fannin is informed that 1,000 Mexicans led by General José Urrea are only two days' march from Goliad. He orders his troops to return with haste to defend the fort. At the Alamo, Travis, now desperate, sends Juan Seguin and Antonio Arocha to Gonzales and on to the Convention at Washington-on-the-Brazos for help.

MARCH 1, 3 A.M. A force of 32 volunteers from the settlement of Gonzales break through the Mexican lines, and into the Alamo.

MARCH 2. At Washington-on-the-Brazos, delegates to the Convention declare Texas independent.

MARCH 3, 11 A.M. After four days, Bonham returns with word that Fannin will not come to the aid of the Alamo. That evening Travis sends John W. Smith to the Convention with a final plea for aid.

MARCH 4. Early in the morning Santa Anna calls a council to discuss storming the Alamo, but no definite time is set for the assault. Later in the day, a Mexican battery shatters a section of the Alamo's north wall. The west wall is under constant fire from cannon across the river.

At the Convention, David G. Burnet is appointed provisional President, and Sam Houston is named Commander-in-Chief of all Texas land forces.

MARCH 5. By dawn the Mexican battery from the north has pushed to within 200 yards of the Alamo. Mexican fire is now heavy and continuous.

2 P.M. Santa Anna outlines to his officers a plan for the final assault. Attack will be launched simultaneously from the northwest (Cós), northeast (Duque), east (Romero), and south (Morales).

That night, the Mexican General silences his military bands, thus granting the Texans inside the Alamo a few precious hours of sleep.

MARCH 6. Just after 5 A.M. the Mexicans storm forward. After two unsuccessful assaults they flood into the fort and overwhelm the Texans. Travis, manning the fort's north cannon, is shot through the head; Crockett is killed defending his post (the actual details of his death have never been verified). Mexicans armed with bayonets rush to Bowie's cot in the chapel sacristy and stab him repeatedly until he is dead. By 6:40 A.M. the battle is over. All 187 defenders have been slain. More than 1,000 Mexicans have been killed or wounded. At 8 A.M. Santa Anna sends the official report of victory to Mexico City.

MARCH 11. Houston arrives at Gonzales and begins forming his army. That night he learns of the Alamo's fall from two Mexicans. To avert panic he denies the report and has the informers jailed as spies. Fannin is ordered to retreat to Victoria, but refuses.

MARCH 12. Houston orders townspeople at Gonzales to burn the settlement to the ground and begin a long retreat to the east.

MARCH 19. Fannin, finally deciding to withdraw, is overtaken and defeated by General Urrea. He and his troops are marched back to Goliad, expecting to be paroled.

MARCH 27. All of Fannin's men are killed at Santa Anna's order.

While Houston and his growing forces retreat eastward toward Louisiana, Santa Anna sets out in pursuit of President Burnet and his Cabinet, who are fleeing toward Galveston. The chase ranges over the plain of San Jacinto. Houston, seeing a chance to trap the Mexicans, speeds toward the plain with a force of 800, reaching Buffalo Bayou on April 19th.

APRIL 21. General Cós, with 500 men, arrives at Santa Anna's camp. A detail of Texans under "Deaf" Smith destroy Vince's Bridge, trapping the Mexicans on the plain and cutting them off from further reinforcements.

4 P.M. Houston attacks the enemy and in a matter of minutes achieves a victory. Crying "Remember the Alamo! Remember Goliad!" the Texans kill 630 Mexicans and wound 200 more. Seven hundred and fifty Mexicans are taken prisoner. Texan losses amount to 9 killed and 30 wounded.

MAY 14. Houston forces Santa Anna to sign treaties recognizing Texas independence and agreeing to remove his troops from Texas.

SEPTEMBER. The Texas Constitution is ratified in a general election. Sam Houston is elected the first President of the Republic.

Dawn, March 6, 1836: the siege of the Alamo at its grim climax

3

The Final Victory

WHILE the defenders were fighting for their lives at the Alamo, everything was going well at the Convention.

On March 2nd, the delegates drafted the Declaration of Independence. Four days later scout John W. Smith rode into Washington-on-the-Brazos, bearing Travis' last appeal for help. He had left the Alamo on March 3rd, the tenth day of the siege.

Sam Houston left to go to the rescue of the Alamo. He headed for Gonzales to assemble the volunteers there and unite them with Fannin's five hundred. A courier had already ridden ahead with orders to Fannin to join him.

A few hours after his departure, Houston stopped, got down from his horse, cupped his ear to the earth and listened as he had learned to do from the Cherokees. When he got up his face was solemn. He announced that firing at the Alamo had ceased. Nevertheless, he kept on.

He found out for sure as soon as he reached Gonzales on March 11th.

Shortly after his arrival, two Mexicans from San Antonio rode into town shouting that the Alamo had fallen, and all its defenders had been killed. Horror and panic swept the settlement. Many women of Gonzales were widowed, their children left fatherless.

Houston knew the report was probably true. But he had to rally the 374 volunteers before their spirits fell; he also had to withhold the news from the other "Anglo" colonies until he could put an army between the settlements and Santa Anna. For these reasons the report had to be denied. Houston ordered the arrest of the Mexican newsbearers as spies.

He waited for Fannin, but Fannin did not come. In this crisis, Houston was forced to retreat. He sent Fannin another order, this time to blow up the fort at Goliad and join him, twenty miles to the east, at Victoria.

But Houston was unable to keep his secret any longer. The next day, Susannah Dickinson came home to Gonzales and gave the Texans a full, horrifying eyewitness account of the slaughter. Santa Anna had spared her life for this precise purpose.

Houston tried his best to keep the news confined to Gonzales; but before he could check them, several of the settlers had ridden away to warn friends and kin in the colonies. Now Houston had on his hands a terrified and fleeing civilian population which he had somehow to control at the same time that he was whipping the raw volunteers into an army. To impede the expected Mexican advance, he ordered Gonzales burned to the ground.

Houston assigned all the wagons to transport the civilians. For the rest of the campaign, his army had to carry with them the hungry and frightened women and children and old men who had lost their homes and had nowhere to go and who did not dare linger in their undefended towns. The force at his command, which was now the only army in existence, numbered no more than 500 fighting men, aside from the company at Goliad under Colonel Fannin.

General Houston (San Jacinto Museum of History Association)

"Runaway Scrape"

Fortunately for the Texans, Santa Anna rested on his laurels. He assumed that all resistance would end with the Alamo. Meanwhile, he was rebuilding his army by recruiting volunteers from among the Mexicans in Texas to replace his dead and wounded. And he had to give his men a rest.

Houston, retreating eastward in the direction of the United States border (Louisiana was two hundred miles away), had three purposes in mind, although he thought it best to keep them to himself. For one, he wanted to help the escaping families get away to Louisiana. For another, he wanted to add every last possible recruit to his army before engaging in the inevitable all-out battle with Santa Anna's superior forces. And, third, he hoped to scatter and divide the pursuing Mexican army. But he needed time.

The weather gave him that time. Spring rains came down in torrents. Rivers flooded; bridges were washed out; roads became quagmires. Fortunately, these unforeseen developments impeded Santa Anna more than they did the Texans.

Because Houston kept his plans secret, consulting no one, his officers and men grew daily more furious. They were burning to avenge the Alamo. But Houston's patience was monumental. He insisted on more drill, on waiting for artillery from the States, on waiting for the American volunteers who, he was certain, would hurry to his aid as soon as news of the Alamo reached the States.

So he kept on retreating east, drilling and resting his army at plantations and farms on the way, many of them abandoned in the civilian "Runaway Scrape" as it was called. Luckily, in their haste, they had left behind them cows, chickens, grain and stables with stores, all badly needed by a hungry army.

But Houston's fighting force, although growing, was now on the brink of mutiny. Weren't his men sworn to defend these homes instead of abandoning them to the ruin of Santa Anna's scorched-earth policy?

Houston didn't bother to justify his plan. No one had listened to him in the clutch of the last crisis; why should he waste his time in trying to explain now?

Reports from his scouts convinced him that his tactics were working. Gradually they were causing the Mexican Army, baffled by his movements, to fan out.

Santa Anna sent one wing of his army under General Jóse Urrea, up the Gulf Coast. To cover the north, he dispatched General Rafael Gaona's troops to Nacogdoches. He himself

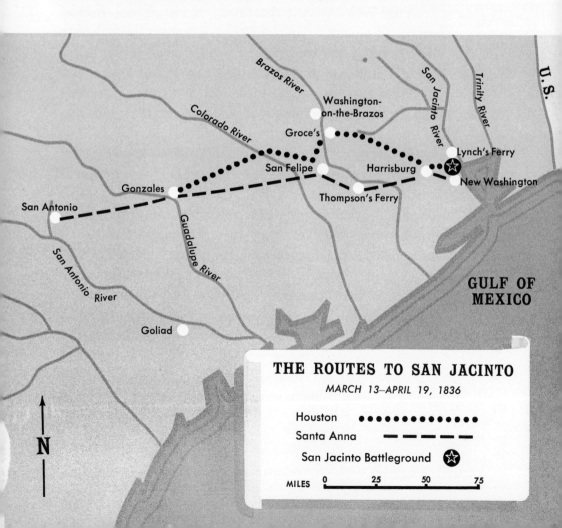

THE ROUTES TO SAN JACINTO

MARCH 13–APRIL 19, 1836

Houston ●●●●●●●●●●●●

Santa Anna – – – – – –

San Jacinto Battleground ✪

MILES 0 25 50 75

would lead the main army, thrusting eastward from San Antonio.

If Houston could keep these three wings apart while he pursued each in turn, he had at least a fighting chance of beating them.

Engagement at Coleto Creek

Fannin, at Goliad, had so far ignored Houston's order of March 13th to retreat to Victoria.

By March 19th, Urrea was before Goliad with 1,500 men. Fannin at last started out—much too late—to join Houston's army. That afternoon, General Urrea caught up with him at Coleto Creek. Against the advice of his officers, Fannin engaged the enemy on an open plain, whereas if he had gone on another two or three miles, he would have had the shelter of a wood and a source of water, which he needed desperately.

Forming his men into a sort of walled square, with fieldpieces at the four corners, Fannin gave battle. Urrea had better guns and three times as many troops. It was a brave but senseless action. The Texans groaned for water; the unswabbed cannon got too hot to handle; the wounded could not be cared for.

Nightfall gave Fannin's men a brief reprieve. But when morning came they saw that their situation was hopeless. Fannin called a council. It was agreed to surrender on certain terms. Urrea, a humane general, accepted, and promised to return the men to the States (nearly all of Fannin's soldiers were courageous young volunteers from the Old South).

Urrea kept these men locked up for a week at Goliad. When Santa Anna heard of it, he flew into a rage, countermanded the terms of surrender and ordered Urrea to shoot them all. In his war, there would be no prisoners.

On Palm Sunday, March 27th, the captive Texans were marched twenty miles down the road leading to Copano Bay, thinking that they were about to be put aboard ship and sent back home, as promised.

Suddenly, a Mexican officer raised his arm. A volley rang out. They were shot down from behind. Fannin escaped the first blast. He had a chance to ask to be buried and not to be shot head on, but his face was ripped to shreds by gunfire; he was not buried but left for the prairie wolves. Santa Anna was behaving true to form.

Hunter and Hunted

The Mexican General had been unable to lure the wary and elusive Houston into a fight. Now he decided instead to seize the fleeing Texas "government." Learning that President David Burnet with his Cabinet was fleeing toward Galveston, he picked 800 men and set out in pursuit. He barely missed catching his quarry, first at Harrisburg (now part of present-day Houston), then at New Washington on the western shore of Galveston Bay.

Yet, in a curious way, Burnet's mad scramble to escape capture led to the turning point of the war. The pursuing Santa Anna kept zigzagging over the peninsula of San Jacinto, a water-locked plain, which had only two approaches. One was at Vince's Bridge on the northwest corner; the other was at Lynch's Ferry, to the northeast.

Finally, Sam Houston saw his chance and made up his mind. Once he had done so, he moved with relentless speed to trap Santa Anna with 800 men in the network of streams and bayous around San Jacinto. He kept his forces on the move until, near midnight on April 19th, they reached Buffalo Bayou.

Here they paused long enough to tear down a log cabin to make rafts for floating their supplies—among them two cannons known as the "Twin Sisters"—across the river.

The men were exhausted. But as soon as they reached the other side Houston ordered them forward again. His strategy was to seize control of Lynch's Ferry, and so close one of the two exits from the plain.

When, at last, he let his men pitch camp in the moonlight, he was no longer the hunted.

He was the hunter.

Next morning, April 20th, the Texans woke to find that they were on a high prairie surrounded by the bay. It was a peaceful scene. On every side, ranch cows grazed contentedly. Houston ordered a roundup; his men, hungry for so long, would eat steak for breakfast.

But as the barbecue was being prepared, the sound of gun-

On March 27, 1836, Urrea's troops massacre Fannin and his men.

fire rattled over the plain. A few minutes later, "Deaf" Smith and other scouts rode in to say that they had encountered a unit of Santa Anna's outriders. The Texans had been spotted. Battle was imminent.

Houston moved his men into a protecting grove of trees, then he stationed the two six-pounders just inside its outer edge. He now held an advantageous position. To have attained it was worth all the strain.

If Santa Anna intended to cross by the ferry, the Texans would be able to draw a perfect bead on his line of march. If he meant to attack, Houston's men could shoot from the grove and from the treetops.

On the Battleground

Santa Anna soon made his intentions clear. Shortly after noon, the Mexican Army displayed its might by appearing in grand parade,with regimental bands, in front of the woods half a mile away.

The Texans were impressed. They could not but admire the maneuvers of the well-trained cavalry, the shining brass of the artillery, the long lines of supply wagons, the steel of the lancers gleaming in the sunshine. Compared with their own muddy and bedraggled forces, the well-drilled Mexican phalanx looked unbeatably professional.

Santa Anna hoped, as he reported later, "to lure the land thieves out of the trees." He thought the parade would do the trick. But the Texans weren't so simple-minded. They refused the bait. Sam Houston was setting the traps, not walking into them.

As though to entice the Texans into the open, Mexican musketeers fired a volley. Then another—and another. But no head showed; no Texan ran out. Then Santa Anna set up his twelve-pounder. From only three hundred yards away, he began to lob cannon balls into the grove. Still no reaction.

Recalling, perhaps, his victory at the Alamo, Santa Anna ordered the bands to play the "cut-throat" *Degüello*.

The Texas cannoneers now fired some blasts of their own. The noise was effective, but that was all; their ammunition, alas, consisted only of fragments of horseshoes. The shots did not carry very far.

With his flair for the dramatic, the Mexican General ordered his twelve-pounder advanced fifty yards into the open, then rode out with it, on a bay horse, wearing his medals and his Napoleonic hat. This gesture of bravado prompted General Castrillón to protest: "Your Excellency, this is a good way to lose a war we've already won."

Santa Anna ignored his warning. Just then the shooting began. In a few minutes, each side scored a hit. The Mexicans wounded Colonel Neill, the Texan artillery commander and a veteran of the assault on San Antonio. A ball from one of the "Twin Sisters" struck a young Mexican captain at Santa Anna's side, narrowly missing the General himself.

Shortly before, Santa Anna had sent a courier to General Cós to bring up 500 men in reinforcement. While awaiting Cós's arrival, he ordered his men to pitch camp in timber opposite the Texans.

It was a quiet night, although both camps were on the alert. Sam Houston was up very late. He sat on a campstool by himself, lost in thought.

At nine o'clock the next morning, April 21st, General Cós and his 500 men crossed over Vince's Bridge and came into camp unchallenged. Cós's men, like Houston's before them, had marched all night. They stacked arms in a nearby grove and lay down to catch up on their sleep.

It was "Deaf" Smith who told Houston Cós had come.

Detail of Texan flag that flew at the Battle of San Jacinto

Sam listened to him, then ordered him to take a detail and demolish the bridge. Santa Anna was cut off from any possible reinforcements.

Now it had to be a fight to the finish; nobody could get in—or out. The Mexican Army had about 1,500 men to Houston's 800—odds of almost two to one.

The Battle of San Jacinto

The day was wonderfully bright and clear.

At noon Houston summoned his field officers for a council of war, the first and only one that he held during the entire campaign. It lasted for two hours. These were the men who had for so long been bitterly critical of Houston's policy of retreat.

This time they were gathered to discuss attack. To Sam's surprise, now that they had their chance, they could not seem to make up their minds. He let them talk on.

Then, at three o'clock in the afternoon he suddenly ordered the troops to prepare themselves. Lookouts posted in the tree-tops with glasses reported that they could detect no signs of life around the Mexican camp. The entire army appeared to be enjoying a long siesta, a midday rest. The lookouts could not even spot any sentinels.

This was the moment.

The Texas Army spread out, two deep, its formation extending for a length of more than nine hundred yards. General Houston rode up and down the line, passing inspection and giving last-minute instructions.

Then, taking the lead, he raised his sword, steadied his horse Saracen, and, booming out the order "Forward—march!" he dashed ahead. The ringing command was transmitted jubilantly all down the line. After their long retreat, the only problem now was to hold the Texans in check. As they advanced through the tall grass, Houston had to shout to his men, "Hold your fire! Hold your fire!"

The main encampment of Mexicans was only six hundred yards away as the forward movement began. Most of the enemy were still asleep. The Texas column was some three hundred yards off when artillery and rifle fire burst upon it. Sentries, although unseen by the lookouts, had been posted after all. Houston sternly repeated his command, again and again.

Only when the Texans were within forty yards of the Mexican breastworks, an improvised redoubt made of fallen trees, carts, boxes, mounds of dirt, did Houston at last give the order to fire. At this moment, the Texans' band, consisting in its entirety of two or three fifers and one drummer, broke into a popular song of the day, "Come to the Bower." It was the least martial of music.

The "Twin Sisters," which the artillerymen had been haul-

ing a few yards in advance of the infantry, barked forth.
The range was so short that, feeble as it was, this time the
shot tore a hole in the Mexican breastworks. The Texans
swarmed through the opening, shouting the battle cry in
which Houston had briefed them two days earlier: "Remember the Alamo! Remember Goliad!"

By the time they were inside the breastworks among the
astonished Mexicans, Sam Houston was on his third horse.
Two had already been shot from under him.

The fighting lasted no more than twenty minutes. The
Mexicans resisted bravely; General Castrillón set an example
by leaping to the top of a wagon and shouting commands
from that exposed position. But he was shot down before his
shouts could rally the troops from their confusion.

Most of them were running for their guns which they had
stacked for the siesta when the attackers fell upon them.
Every Texan fought for himself, shouting "Remember the
Alamo!" and killing without mercy. Few officers were able
to keep any semblance of control. It was a rout, and venge-
ance ruled the day. Houston himself, although wounded in
the foot early in the fray, kept on fighting until resistance
was broken.

Very few Mexicans escaped the Texans' fury; but one who
did was Santa Anna himself. At the first sound of the attack,
he dashed out of his canopied tent. One look told him that
nothing could be salvaged from the disaster at San Jacinto,
unless he saved himself. He was right. He leaped quickly
on a black charger to ride to Filisola's camp on the Brazos
River for help. On the trackless prairie, he could only guess
at directions.

The battle was over. The Mexicans had lost 630 men, with
200 more badly wounded and about 750 taken prisoner. Four
hundred of the latter owed their lives to Colonel Juan Al-

monte, Santa Anna's personal secretary, who swiftly surveyed the situation for what it was and adroitly withdrew his men from the conflict.

The Mexican prisoners feared for their lives; long after the gunfire had ended they kept shouting in terror "Me no Alamo! Me no Goliad!"

That night when the Texans built bonfires to dry out their clothes and gear, the Mexicans corralled in a stockade were sure the blazes were funeral pyres being prepared for them.

Only later did the prisoners realize they would be treated humanely under a civilized code of warfare—one that Santa Anna himself had violated.

Aftermath

Santa Anna's time was running out. At dawn on April 22, 1836, details of Texas scouts were scouring the neighborhood around Buffalo Bayou and the San Jacinto River to track him down. Meanwhile, Houston—his wounded leg attended to for the moment—could afford to wait.

Every now and then, he popped grains of parched corn into his mouth, offering some to the soldiers standing guard. The men stared idly across the mile-wide battlefield of San Jacinto. Then, from the distance, six horsemen appeared— five Texan, one Mexican. Had Houston's scouts known the identity of their prisoner, he might not have been left alive to surrender. But alive he was, the embodiment of the Mexican Government, as well as its military commander-in-chief. The Napoleon of the West was at last in Houston's hands.

Considering the brutality of his ways, Santa Anna's treatment from Houston was remarkably lenient. His life was spared, and he was held as a prisoner. He secured his release by signing a treaty recognizing the independence of Texas.

To Vince's Bridge

Buffalo Bayou

San Jacinto River

HOUSTON'S CAMP

BURLESON   ARTILLERY AND REGULARS   SHERMAN

MAIN ARMY UNDER SANTA ANNA

SANTA ANNA'S CAMP

ALMONTE

San Jacinto Bay

Marsh

N

THE BATTLE OF SAN JACINTO
4 P.M., APRIL 21, 1836

Santa Anna delivers his speech of surrender to General Houston.

Later, Mexico repudiated the treaty and suspended his dictatorship.

But his fantastic career was far from ended. He was later recalled to the presidency, and over many years alternated between holding positions of power and being forced to seek refuge in the United States or other countries. During the United States–Mexican War, he fought against General Taylor at the Battle of Buena Vista.

Santa Anna spent his last days in poverty and obscurity in his own country, where he returned after having been granted an amnesty in 1874. He died in Mexico City on June 20, 1876, forty years after the Alamo massacre.

Houston, a hero once more because of his victory, resumed his career in public life, and became, as he had once prophesied, President of the Republic of Texas.

The Texas War of Independence covered only five or six months of fighting; it involved only five or six small battles, five or six heroic leaders, and on the Texan side, only some two thousand fighting men. Many campaigns in American history involved many more troops and lasted longer. But the two famous battles of this war—the resistance at the Alamo and victory at San Jacinto—stand out in the story of our nation for two reasons. They are symbols of great courage and great purpose; and, most important of all, their successful outcome removed the last obstacle to creating a unified nation on the North American continent.

FOR FURTHER READING

DOUGLAS, CLAUDE LEROY. *James Bowie, the Life of a Bravo*. Dallas, Texas: B. Upshaw, 1944.

HALL-QUEST, OLGA. *Shrine of Liberty, the Alamo*. New York: Dutton, 1948.

JAMES, MARQUIS. *The Raven: A Biography of Sam Houston*. New York: Paperback Library.

LORD, WALTER. *A Time to Stand*. New York: Harper, 1961.

MYERS, JOHN. *The Alamo*. New York: Dutton, 1948.

RICHARDSON, RUPERT N. *Texas, the Lone Star State*. Englewood Cliffs, N.J.: Prentice-Hall, 1943.

ROURKE, CONSTANCE. *Davy Crockett*. New York: Harcourt, 1934.

SHACKFORD, JAMES. *David Crockett, the Man and the Legend*. Chapel Hill, N.C.: University of North Carolina Press, 1956.

SUTHERLAND, JOHN. *The Fall of the Alamo*. San Antonio, Texas: Naylor, 1936.

TINKLE, LON. *Thirteen Days to Glory*. New York: McGraw-Hill, 1958.

TOLBERT, FRANK. *The Day of San Jacinto*. New York: McGraw-Hill, 1959.

WARREN, ROBERT PENN. *Remember the Alamo!* New York: Random House, 1948.

ZAVALA, ADINA DE. *The Alamo: Where the Last Man Died*. San Antonio, Texas: Naylor, 1956.

INDEX